Cecily Bonville-Grey, Marchioness of Dorset

From Riches to Royalty

Cecily Bonville-Grey, Marchioness of Dorset

From Riches to Royalty

Sarah J. Hodder

Winchester, UK
Washington, USA

JOHN HUNT PUBLISHING

First published by Chronos Books, 2022
Chronos Books is an imprint of John Hunt Publishing Ltd., No. 3 East St., Alresford,
Hampshire SO24 9EE, UK
office@jhpbooks.com
www.johnhuntpublishing.com
www.chronosbooks.com

For distributor details and how to order please visit the 'Ordering' section on our website.

ISBN: 978 1 78904 902 2
978 1 78904 903 9 (ebook)
Library of Congress Control Number: 2021932922

A CIP catalogue record for this book is available from the British Library.

Design: Stuart Davies

UK: Printed and bound by CPI Group (UK) Ltd, Croydon, CR0 4YY
Printed in North America by CPI GPS partners

We operate a distinctive and ethical publishing philosophy in
all areas of our business, from our global network of authors to
production and worldwide distribution.

Contents

Also by Sarah J. Hodder

The Queen's Sisters – The Lives of the Sisters of Elizabeth Woodville. Chronos Books, March 2020.
The York Princesses. Chronos Books, April 2021.

Chapter One

The Early Years at Shute

1459-1462

Set high up on a hill and just four miles from the beautiful Devon coastline, Shute manor house was surrounded by lush green countryside. It was in this quintessential stone building, with its prime views of the wide Devon valleys and with the river Coly bubbling away in the distance, that Cecily Bonville was born, in about 1459/60. At the time of her birth, England was a troubled land, dominated by the ongoing rivalry between the two great houses of York and Lancaster. The period we now know as the Wars of the Roses began just a mere few years before Cecily's birth, although for the troubles that lasted for nigh on thirty years, there was no formal start date. But by the time the infant Cecily made her way into the world, tensions were rising, and lines had already begun to be drawn between the great and noble families of the land. And at the heart of the troubles was nothing less than the throne of England.

Cecily was the first daughter born to William Bonville and his wife Katherine, and unbeknownst to them at the time, she would be the only child they had together. Within a few days of her birth, she would have been christened at the small church situated just behind the manor house and at a time when childbirth was precarious to both mother and child, the family would no doubt have given thanks for her safe arrival into the world. The first few months of her life would have been spent safe in her cradle, wrapped in her swaddling bands to keep her warm and ensure her tiny limbs formed correctly, entirely oblivious to the troubled world she had been born into.

England's ruling monarch at the time of Cecily's birth was Henry VI. Henry had ascended to the throne as a mere infant himself; his father had died in 1422 when Henry was just nine months old. Due to his tender years, a regency council was formed to rule in the king's name until he was old enough to do so himself. The council was headed up by his uncles, John, Duke of Bedford and Humphrey, Duke of Gloucester.

Henry VI would no doubt have grown up in the shadow of his greatly respected father, knowing as he grew into his kingship that he had much to live up to. His father, Henry V, the great warrior king, was arguably one of the most impressive rulers of the House of Plantagenet. His legendary reputation began during his lifetime and has travelled down the centuries. Both to his contemporaries and to history, Henry V was a hero. With an unwavering zeal to revive the claim of his great-grandfather, Edward III, to reclaim French territory and bring it back under English control, he relentlessly pursued his goal to seat himself upon the throne of France. Henry ascended the throne in 1413 at the age of twenty-seven and by 1415 he had begun his quest, crossing the channel and leading an English army into French territory. On 25th of October that year, in an epic battle reminiscent of David and Goliath, his small, and by then exhausted army of an estimated 8,000 troops defeated a much larger French army in a mighty victory at Agincourt.

With a renewed determination, Henry then continued his advancement through France, eventually negotiating a treaty in 1420 with the French king, Charles VI. In what became known as the Treaty of Troyes, Henry V took Charles daughter, Catherine of Valois, as his bride, and Charles agreed to name Henry as heir apparent to the French throne. However just two years later Henry was dead, sadly rendering truth to the words of his brother, the Duke of Bedford, who had once said of Henry that he was 'too famous to live long'. Aged just thirty-five years old, Henry died in the land he was so determined to conquer, most likely from dysentery. During his nine years on the English throne, he had achieved much of his goal, having brought back a good proportion of French territory under English rule.

From 1422 until 1437 England remained under the protectorate of the Dukes of Gloucester and Bedford – the Duke of Gloucester remaining in England and the Duke of Bedford overseeing English territories in northern France. But in 1437, at the age of fifteen, Henry VI was finally considered old enough to take over the reins of Government. But the new king's temperament was nothing like his father's; if Henry V was the warrior king, Henry VI was his antithesis in every way. A contemporary of Henry's, John Blacman, who served for a while as his chaplain and later became his biographer, described him as 'a simple man, without any crook of craft or untruth as is plain to all. With none did he deal craftily, nor ever would say an untrue word to any, but framed his speech always to speak the truth'. Blacman goes on to tell us that in all things Henry liked a simple way of living and that it was 'well known that from his youth up he always wore round-toed shoes and boots like a farmer's. He also customarily wore a long gown with a rolled hood like a townsman, and a full coat reaching below his knees'.[1]

Instead of being a strong and influential leader, it seems that Henry saw himself fulfilling the role of a kind father to his subjects, their mentor rather than their champion. The passion that his father had shown in invading France was not echoed by his son and by the end of Henry VI's reign, all English land in France, with the exception of the port and town of Calais, had been lost once more. Blacman reports 'The same prince when in the end he lost both the realms, England and France, which he had ruled before, along with all his wealth and goods, endured it with no broken spirit but with a calm mind, making light of all temporal things, if he might but gain Christ and things eternal'.

In 1445, aged twenty-three, Henry had married; his new bride, Margaret of Anjou, was a niece of the French king, and the union secured a peace with France. Whether the couple were compatible is debatable, but her loyalty was never in doubt and in later years Margaret would fight fiercely in defence of her husband and her throne.

As well as bringing about peace between the two nations, the job of the new queen was to produce an heir. This she did in 1453 when she gave birth to their first son, whom they named Edward. However, just before his birth, Henry fell into a strange state of depression, that royal physicians were unable to diagnose. It came on suddenly and rendered him into a coma-like state – awake but completely unresponsive. When his only son and heir was born, Henry could not even recognise him despite the attempts of the Duke of Buckingham and the queen, who presented the prince to him at Windsor, begging the king to bless the prince, thereby giving official recognition to his son. Glancing upon the tiny baby boy, he lowered his eyes to the floor, showing no reaction. Doubts very quickly began to be raised on his effectiveness to rule. Before he may have been deemed quite an ineffectual ruler, but now it seemed he was in no fit state to rule at all.

By January the following year he did not seem to be making any recovery and Queen Margaret, keen to safeguard herself and her baby son, made a case for her to rule as Regent until her husband was fully recovered. England, however, was not yet ready for a female ruler and her case was rejected. The council instead elected a Protector, someone who would act as a caretaker of the realm until the king was well again. The man they chose for the role was Richard Plantagenet, Duke of York, who at this time, was the foremost Duke in the land. A descendant of Edward III, through two family lines – his father was the son of Edmund, the 1st Duke of York and fourth son of Edward III, and his mother was a great-granddaughter of Lionel, Duke of Clarence, the second of Edward III's sons.

As the months passed, it became clear that Henry VI's mental state was not improving as he wavered between periods of lucidity and periods of depression. As tensions arose between Queen Margaret and her allies and the Duke of York and his supporters, calls were made for Henry's complete removal from the throne; the Duke's supporters arguing that it was now clear that the king was not up to the task. Tensions were rising and sides were being chosen. By 1455 civil war had broken out between the two camps: the Lancastrians – those who remained loyal to the king and his family, and the Yorkists – those who came out in favour of replacing the weak and ill Henry VI with a stronger leader, in the shape of the Duke of York. 1455 had seen the first real combat between the two sides, when the two armies had fought a pitched battle through the streets of St Albans. This had been followed by four years of an uneasy truce, and by 1459 when Cecily made her appearance into the world, tensions were escalating again. By the end of 1459, the Duke of York and his allies had fled England for the continent to regroup and consider their next move. Like all the other great and noble families of the land, Cecily's parents and grandparents would have been well aware of the political situation and found themselves having to pledge their allegiance to one side or the other.

Cecily's mother, Katherine, was a younger daughter of the great Neville family who were related to the Duke of York through marriage. Katherine's father (Cecily's maternal grandfather) was Richard Neville, Earl of Salisbury. His sister, Cecily Neville, had married Richard Duke of York in 1429 and Katherine was therefore his niece. That the Nevilles were Yorkist supporters is perhaps unsurprising.

The Nevilles were a distinguished family, who also had roots back to Edward III through his son, John of Gaunt. Richard Neville was the eldest son of Sir Ralph Neville, the first Earl of Westmorland, by his second wife Lady Joan Beaufort. Joan was the daughter of John of Gaunt and Katherine Swynford. Richard had married Lady Alice Montacute, the daughter and heir of Sir

Thomas de Montacute and it was through her lineage that he acquired the title of Earl of Salisbury in 1428, upon the death of Alice's father.

Born around 1400, Salisbury was in his mid-fifties when the troubles began. He was ably supported in his championing of his brother-in-law, the Duke of York, by his eldest son, also named Richard. Born c.1428, Richard was about fourteen years older than his younger sister Katherine whose birth date is thought to be sometime before 1442. By the time the troubles began, the younger Richard Neville was becoming an influential military man who would later earn himself the name 'the kingmaker'. He would also become much better known as the Earl of Warwick, a title he acquired through his betrothal to Lady Anne Beauchamp, daughter of Richard de Beauchamp, 13th Earl of Warwick. With a Neville as her mother, Cecily had been born into one of the greatest families in the land. But it was from her father, William Bonville, Lord Harington, that she would receive her inheritance that would see her become one of the richest heiresses in England.

Katherine and William had married in 1458, when he was nineteen and she would have been around the age of sixteen. Where the ceremony took place is unknown, but we can assume that it was to Shute manor that the young Katherine went to live after the wedding. Her new husband was descended from a long line of Bonvilles; the family most likely having arrived in England from Bonvil in Normandy sometime in the twelfth century and settling in Devon. The Bonville name can be traced back to a Nicholas de Bonvil who it is thought to have lived at Wiscombe during the reign of King John.[2]

At some point during the thirteenth and fourteenth centuries, later generations of Bonvilles had relocated from Wiscombe to Shute. It was an earlier William Bonville, a great-great-grandson of Nicholas, who built Shute manor house and made it his primary home. This was the house that Cecily would be born into and that she would remain attached to throughout her life. The manor was completed between 1375 and 1407.

At the time of Cecily's birth, three generations of Bonville men were still living, the most prominent of which was old Lord William Bonville, the grandson of the William who built the manor house (the name along with the manor travelled down the ages). This Lord William, who was born in 1392, was Cecily's paternal great-grandfather.

When the troubles began in the 1450s-60s, Lord William and his family were loyal subjects of their king. Aligning themselves through marriage to the Neville family in the late 1450s may have been the first indication that their allegiance to the king was already wavering. But openly they still supported Henry VI. Born to a Yorkist mother and a Lancastrian father, Cecily truly was a War of the Roses child.

Where the Nevilles had strong foundations in the English nobility, the Bonvilles had had to work their way to prominence. Earlier generations had not really made their mark and it was Cecily's great-grandfather, old Lord Bonville, who had really propelled the family into the kind of circles that would facilitate a marriage with a family like the Nevilles. Lord Bonville had inherited the manor of Shute upon the death of his father in 1396, when he was around four years old. An interesting account from his youth comes from 1428, when he would have been around thirty-six years old. On the 14th April of that year Nicholas Wysbeche, Abbot of Newenham, was asked to mediate in a dispute between William and his neighbour, a lady called Joan Brooke, concerning the obstruction of some of the local public roads and paths by Joan and her son. The Abbots ruling went wholly in William's favour and Joan was directed to ensure that all routes be kept clear. But further than that, the Abbot wanted to ensure that there would be no lasting enmity between the neighbours and ordered that 'the knight and the lady should ride amicably together to Newenham Abbey on a day appointed, where they should exchange a kiss in token of peace and friendship and dine together at the abbot's table'.[3] The deed detailing the Abbot's ruling is dated at Axminster 13th August 1428. Whether this did restore a friendship between the pair or whether they simply managed to act their way through the meal went unrecorded!

The vast inheritance that would eventually come to Cecily, came into the family through Lord William's second marriage. His first wife was a lady named Margaret Meriet, with whom he had a son – another William, Cecily's grandfather – and two daughters, Philippa and Margaret. After Margaret died, he took as his second wife Elizabeth Courtenay, the widow of Sir John Harington. She bought with her to the marriage a good proportion of the Harington fortune.

The Harington estates were vast and included lands in Leicestershire, near the famous Crowland (Croyland) Abbey, where the chronicles were compiled. After his marriage, Lord William took charge of these estates, and soon found himself in a dispute with the Abbey on behalf of his tenants. Details of the quarrel were recorded by the unidentified writer of the First Continuation of the Chronicle (who is believed to have been one of the priors at the Abbey). Writing in 1433 he describes William as a 'certain noble and influential Knight of Cornwall'. The writer first notes that 'William Bondvyll, has at this time taken to wife the Lady Elizabeth, relict of the Lord Robert (sic) Haryngton, the Late Lord of Multon. Through marriage the chief demesne of the manor of Multon [now Moulton] came to the said Knight'.[4]

The writer then continues his tale, reporting how the inhabitants of the town had complained to William because their meadows and pastures were being ruined by constant flooding from the precincts of the abbey. It seems the embankment surrounding the Abbey needed repairing and the villagers of Multon were continuously finding their lands swamped, resulting in ruined profits. The consequences of this meant they were unable to pay their rent. In defence of his tenants (and no doubt in defence of his lack of rents), William angrily tackled the Abbot, John Litlington, who did all he could to defend himself. After much expense, a meeting was set up to decide the matter, overseen by two justices of the common pleas and the chief baron of the exchequer where the issue was amicably discussed, and a satisfactory outcome was reached. The abbot was ordered to raise the embankment and make it good and it was to be his responsibility or that of any future abbots within the next three years to ensure this was done. It was instructed that the embankment must be of sufficient height and maintained for the next forty years to stop the overflowing of water. A clause was inserted however, to allow the abbot some leeway in the likelihood of severe weather.[5]

Elizabeth Courtenay, the woman who William had 'taken to wife' was the daughter of Edward de Courtenay, 3rd Earl of Devon. The Courtenay family would feature prominently at court in the 1480s and onwards, through a later marriage between Katherine of York, a daughter of Edward IV and Elizabeth Woodville, and a William Courtenay. Due to their proximity to each other, it seems a love/hate relationship existed between the Bonvilles and the Courtenays. As two prominent southern families, a rivalry existed between them, although they did intermarry on occasion, as in this instance. Through his marriage to Elizabeth, William now found himself connected to the current Earl, Thomas Courtenay, Elizabeth's nephew, who had inherited the title in 1422, upon the death of his father (Elizabeth's brother). But it appears blood was not thicker than water and family loyalties did nothing to prevent the continuing troubles that kept brewing between the two men.

Lord William's prestige and influence had begun to flourish in his home county in the 1430s and 1440s and he was often called upon to witness charters and assist at local fairs and 'love-days' in both Devon and the neighbouring county of Somerset. His increasing prominence exacerbated the friction between the Bonvilles and the Courtenays and reached boiling point when William was honoured by being awarded the stewardship of the duchy of Cornwall. The Earl of Devon saw this as a personal slight, as he considered this post to be his by right of birth. He immediately petitioned the king, angrily demanding the office of steward for himself. To further exacerbate the situation, he too was sent letters patent granting him the post. With two stewards in position, the Council quickly realised their mistake and immediately informed the Earl, asking him to refrain from any official duties. The Earl chose to ignore their instructions, and before too long widespread disorder had broken out in Devon and Cornwall. Unable to find a resolution that satisfied both parties, the Council decreed that the stewardship should be awarded elsewhere. Furthermore, that the Earl and Lord William should both promise to keep the peace. They agreed to this upon oath, although the Earl, seemingly unbothered by the promise he had made, stubbornly continued to call himself steward.

Despite this temporary peace agreement, tensions continued to simmer between the pair and on more than one occasion either one or both of them were hauled before the king's council and reprimanded about their disputes which on occasion had resulted in actual combat. October 1455 saw an extreme instance of their continuing feud when open warfare broke out once again and Shute manor came under attack. The catalyst this time was the murder of Lord Bonville's lawyer, who was violently attacked and killed by the earl of Devon's sons. The Courtenays followed that up by ransacking a town house in Exeter – one of Lord William's properties – and by laying siege to Powderham castle. The castle was the seat of one of their own, Sir Philip Courtenay, but he was a close friend of

Lord William and therefore his surname counted for nothing in the continuing quarrels. Unable to let this pass, Lord William retaliated and the two sides fought a pitched battle on Clyst Heath where 'moche people wer slayn'. Two days later Shute manor was pillaged by the Earl's men, in which must have been a terrifying time for Elizabeth and the family. It is alleged that the Earl's men secured a great amount of loot from the property, including household items, food, and cattle.[6] As well as these local skirmishes between the two families, there was also now much wider unrest happening across the land. The Earl of Devon, a Yorkist supporter, and Lord Bonville, a staunch Lancastrian at that time, had another reason to continue to antagonise each other.

Born c.1416-17, Lord William's only son, and Cecily's grandfather, was also named William. This William had also married a Harington, taking for his wife sometime around 1440 the daughter of William Lord Harington of Aldingham. William was the brother of Sir John Harington, Elizabeth Courtenay's first husband. William's new bride, confusingly also named Elizabeth, was Sir John's only child and heir, and this union brought more of the Harington fortune into the Bonville family. During their marriage, William bore the courtesy title Lord Harington on behalf of his wife. Together they had a son, another William – Cecily's father. He was born c.1441-42 and when he was just sixteen, his maternal grandfather Lord Harington died, and he inherited the title of 6th Lord Harington, which passed to him as his mother's heir; his mother Elizabeth had also died early, and certainly before 1458 when her father, Lord Harington himself died.

At some point towards the end of the 1450s, and certainly by 1460, as political tensions began to reach boiling point, the Bonville family shifted their allegiance from their king and threw their lot in with the Duke of York. This may have in part been due to the deteriorating health of Henry VI and an understandable concern that the country should have a stable government. But it is also likely that the younger William's marriage to Katherine Neville in 1458 may have had an influence in their decision. By July 1460, although the Duke of York himself remained in Ireland, his eldest son, Edward, along with Warwick and Salisbury had returned from France and faced the Lancastrian army in Northampton. This was the moment the Bonvilles made a complete volte-face when they also turned out at the battle of Northampton, fighting on the side of the Yorkists.

Northampton proved a decisive victory for the Yorkists; Henry VI was captured and taken to London and placed in the tower and Queen Margaret fled to Wales with her young son. Hearing news of the victory, the Duke of York returned to England and the Lancastrians once again met with the Yorkist army, this time at Wakefield in December 1460. The Bonville men once again turned out to fight, and it was during this battle that calamity struck the family. All three Williams had been on the battlefield; Cecily's father, aged just twenty-one, her grandfather and Lord William, her great-grandfather. But the battle ended disastrously for all concerned. Not only was it a huge Yorkist defeat when both the Duke of York and his son, Edmund, were killed, but in a more personal tragedy, alongside them on the battlefield both Cecily's father and grandfather also died.

Old William Bonville was the only Bonville male to survive the fighting. Due to his previous loyalty to Henry VI, he was permitted to return to his Devon manor. In what must have been a sad journey for the old man back to Devon, he returned home to Shute, the bearer of terrible news to the women that waited there. For the young Katherine Neville in particular, the news he bought her was devastating. Not only had she lost her husband and father-in-law, but her own father, the Earl of Salisbury had also lost his life. He had escaped the battlefield but was captured during the night and taken to Pontefract Castle.

Pronounced a traitor, he was taken to the Lancastrian camp and beheaded the next day.[7] One of Katherine's brothers, Sir Thomas Neville, was also killed that day. Fortunately, blessed by her youth, Cecily was cushioned from the trauma of losing her father and both her grandfathers that day, and although she may have grown up with a sadness at their loss, the terrible reality of events would not have greatly affected her at such a young age, and she would have remained blissfully ignorant of the misfortune that had befallen her family.

The feeling of sadness and grief inhabiting Shute manor in early 1461 would have been indescribable. Unable to bury either his son or his grandson, old William Bonville must have keenly felt their loss. The death of the Duke of York could have heralded the end of the conflicts, but the Duke's eldest, Edward, Earl of March, was ready to avenge his father's death. Lord William, possibly feeling he had nothing left to lose, was ready to join Edward in seeking revenge.

At some point before February 1461, Lord William joined Richard Neville, Earl of Warwick in London. Warwick had not been at Wakefield but had remained in London in charge of the king.

On 2nd February 1461, a battle took place at Mortimer's Cross with an army led by Edward; the Yorkists emerged victorious. Back in London, on 8th February, Warwick and Lord Bonville were elected Knights of the Garter.[8] Then taking the captured king with them, they headed north to try and defeat Queen Margaret's army once and for all. The two sides met again at the second battle to take place at St Albans, on 17th February 1461, the result being another disastrous defeat for the Yorkists. Although Lord William once again survived the battle, his luck was running out.

By nightfall, Warwick had realised they were beaten, and he withdrew with his men from the battlefield, leaving behind Henry VI in a tent on the field. In an act that perhaps gives us a glimpse into Lord William's character, while all the rest of the army fled, he remained on the battlefield to protect the old king, the man who had once garnered all his loyalty. Arriving at the scene after the battle, Queen Margaret and her son discovered the helpless king alone in his tent. But on guard nearby were two distinguished Yorkist soldiers: Lord Bonville and Sir Thomas Kyriel, who had chivalrously remained to see that no harm came to him. It was recorded that the king had urged them to protect him under the assurance from him that their lives should be preserved. Despite the king's assurance, Queen Margaret declared both men traitors and they were executed on her orders on 18th February. William Bonville was by then sixty-eight years old.

This act of chivalry on William's part was described by Holinshed:

When the daie was closed, those that were about the king (in number a twenty thousand) hearing how euill their fellowes had sped, began utterlie to despair of the victorie, and so fell without anie long tarriance to running awaie. By reason whereof, the nobles that were about the king, perceiving how the game went, and withall saw no comfort in the king, but rather a good will and affection toward the contrarie part, they withdrew also, leauing the king accompanied by the Lord Bonneuille and Sir Thomas Kiriell of Kent, which vpon assurance of the king's promise, tarried with him and fled not. But their trust deceived them, for at the Queenes departing from Saint Albons they were both beheaded, though contrarie to the mind and promise of her husband[9]

No record exists of Lord Bonville's burial place nor that of his sons. As once again the tragic news filtered back to the quiet backwaters of Devon, this time it was Elizabeth Bonville who would have received it in despair at the loss of her husband.

In an even more distressing turn of events, the Crown ordered that the Bonville estates and goods be confiscated. Thankfully for Elizabeth, Katherine and Cecily, just over a month later in March 1461, on the snow-covered fields of Towton, another bloody battle took place that saw the Yorkists finally emerge triumphant. The Duke of York's son, Edward, Earl of March, who had had himself proclaimed King Edward IV in London just a few days before, was now on the throne and the old King Henry, his wife and son fled to Scotland. In thanks for her husband's support, Edward rewarded Elizabeth Bonville by returning all William's estates to her. Cecily, as the last of the Bonville line, would inherit them all after Elizabeth's death. Through a great tragedy, she had become one of the richest heiresses in the country.

In the space of a few months, three generations of Bonville men had been lost and it was now down to their womenfolk to forge a new life for themselves. For Cecily's mother, Katherine, she had barely had time to be a wife, and now found herself a widow. Still just a young woman, she had already suffered great losses in these wars for the throne. Now with a young toddler to support and raise on her own she must have been fearful for what was to come.

Financially at least the women were supported. Elizabeth Courtenay was assigned a large dower by Edward IV and for a while after her father's death, Cecily and her mother, Katherine, remained at Shute manor, living with Elizabeth. Indeed, Elizabeth continued to live there until her own death eleven years later in 1471. Katherine was granted Cecily's wardship and marriage and a jointure from the Bonville and Harington Estates by Edward IV of 600 marks a year.[10]

Shute manor would always remain Cecily's favoured property and was an ideal place for a young toddler to grow up. Close to the sea, the house was set high up on a hill, overlooking wide valleys and surrounded by a large deer park. The nearby

Shute church was a satellite church of Colyton, which was two miles to the north of the house. Next to the house was a tiny well which provided their water supply. The Bonville women also had access to a huge amount of open space to walk in and use for their leisure. The manor was also well situated for easy routes to Colyford, Somerset, Axminster, Honiton and Exeter, where the elder Lord Bonville had several properties which now by right were theirs.

The house itself was not large by any standards but would have been suitable for a family of their means. The front of the house had a central front door, with a gothic window on each side. Adjoined to the left side of the building was a hexagonal turret, with a staircase that led up to the top floor. The staircase was entered into by another Gothic door and exited at the top by an identical door. The top floor of the house featured an upstairs gallery with two further windows providing the light.[11]

The main feature, as with many houses of the period, was the large open hall which occupied the whole of the ground floor and which was accessed directly from the front door. Upon entering the house, you would immediately be met by the sight of a huge fireplace, spanning the whole width of the building. With open fires commonplace, Cecily, growing up as a toddler, would have been supervised carefully when in the hall. Medieval families were very aware of dangers that could befall young children, so much so that at baptisms godparents were instructed to ensure the parents kept their child safe from fire, water and other perils until he or she was seven years old.[12]

Within the great hall, a raised platform covered about half the floor space upon which was situated a high table where the family would eat. The men and women of the household would eat in the lower part of the hall. Separate outbuildings contained the kitchen and bake house and the manor also contained a pantry and buttery, which were situated within the main hall but separated by screens. The Lord and Lady's chamber and presumably a chamber for young Cecily formed part of the gallery above. The gallery floor extended only over part of the hall below.

Cecily may not have remembered much of her early years here, but she would later return to the manor and make it her home once again. She also had a real fondness for Elizabeth, her great-grandmother, and in later years she would fund a memorial to her. Even though terrible misfortunes had struck Cecily at a young age, her first two years would have been spent much as any infant and toddler, surrounded by the love of her mother and great-grandmother and in an idyllic location. But sometime around the age of two, Cecily and her mother were packing their belongings and getting ready to depart the manor for a new life, as Katherine prepared for a new marriage. Her new husband, and Cecily's new stepfather, William Hastings, brought Cecily even closer into the sphere of the court.

Chapter Two

The Lord Chamberlain's Stepdaughter

1462-1474

The exact date Katherine and William Hastings were married went unrecorded, but it was sometime before February 1462.[1] Katherine's second husband was a close friend of England's new king, Edward IV, and the union would almost certainly have been arranged by her brother, Richard Neville, the Earl of Warwick, perhaps in collusion with the king himself. As the new king's cousin, Warwick was popular with the people, and his support for Edward and his valiant actions in battle to place his cousin on the throne had earned him the name 'the kingmaker'. England had a new young king, and the king had the support of one of the most respected men in England. What could possibly go wrong?

It is difficult to gauge Katherine's personality from a modern perspective so it is impossible to know whether she yearned for a new husband. She was still so young, only just into her twenties, so the expectation would have been for her to marry again; perhaps she may even have welcomed the chance to start a new relationship. But she may also have been quite content living in Devon with her young daughter. Either way, she would have been informed at some point that she had been found a new husband, and that the husband that had been chosen for her was a Leicestershire gentleman named, like her first husband, William. It is quite probable that due to Katherine having spent the last few years in the far-off county of Devon, that the pair were strangers to each other at the time of their marriage.

William Hastings was born around 1430, making him around twelve years older than Katherine. He was the eldest son of

Leonard Hastings and his wife Alice Camoys. Leonard and Alice also had three other sons and three daughters. By the time of William and Katherine's marriage, Leonard had been dead some seven years, having died in October 1455. Alice survived her husband, but it is not known when she died so she may or may not have been there to welcome Katherine and Cecily upon their arrival in Leicestershire.[2]

Hastings' connection and path to becoming a close friend and confidant of the new king began many years earlier through his connections to Edward's father, Richard Duke of York. By 1455, when Hastings was twenty-five years old, he was standing as Sheriff of Burton Hastings in Warwickshire and Kirby Muxloe in Leicestershire. Following in the footsteps of his father, Leonard, William was also a retainer of the Duke of York.

Clearly the Duke of York and his family held Hastings in high esteem. In a Deed dated 23rd April 1456, the Duke addressed William as his 'beloved servant', granting him an annuity of £10, that he should serve him above all others, except the king (referring at that time of course to Henry VI).[3] Hastings' chance to seal his allegiance to the York family came during the troubled years of the 1460s. Uninvolved in earlier battles between the rival houses, in 1461 he assembled and equipped a force to fight on the Yorkist side. Raising an army of men was an expensive undertaking and this would certainly have challenged him financially. He and his group of men joined Edward on the battlefield at Mortimer's Cross in February 1461 where they were part of the resounding victory against the Lancastrian army. With Edward's kingship sealed the following month, after the battle of Towton, the new king was keen to reward those men who had helped him get there. In appreciation of his support to both Edward and his family, Hastings received a knighthood directly after the battle, one of only six gentlemen knighted on the field.[4]

Although they may have been acquaintances or even friends

much earlier than this, from this moment on, William Hastings was to become one of Edward's closest friends, confidant, and general right-hand man. After the battle, Edward and his supporters returned to London and on Sunday 28th June 1461 Edward received his formal coronation at Westminster Abbey. A month later, on 26th July 1461, Hastings was created Baron Hastings of Ashby-de-la-Zouch. The patent confirming his peerage illustrates how highly he was esteemed by Edward:

Calling to mind the honourable service, probity and valiant deeds of our dearly beloved knight William Hastynges, our chamberlain, we wish to raise him to the rank of baron and peer of our realm, as much for his martial exploits as for his good example and good counsel. We particularly single out how the said William with a large force of his servants, friends and well-wishers did at heavy and burdensome cost and manifold peril expose himself most courageously and shrewdly in our service in campaigns and battles against our arch-enemy the former pretended king of England, 'Henry the Sixth', with his accomplices and abettors, notably Jasper Pembroke and James Wiltshire, formerly earls, who together with other traitors and rebels waged war on us. From his early manhood he has never ceased to serve us...[5]

After much bloodshed on both sides, Edward had achieved what his father had set out to do and had removed the weak and troubled King Henry from the throne. He had been assisted by two men who would come to play a huge part in his life, Warwick and William Hastings – Cecily's uncle and soon-to-be stepfather. What relationship there was between Warwick and Hastings early on is undocumented, but Warwick clearly thought highly enough of him to marry him to his younger sister. Their union would mean that it was now time for Katherine and Cecily to pack their bags and leave Shute; their destination would have been the Midlands, probably to Kirby Muxloe, William's family home.

At the time of her mother's second marriage, Cecily was still only a small child. With the resilience of childhood, it is likely she adjusted to this change of residence without too much issue. Arriving in Leicestershire, Katherine and Cecily would have been greeted by the sight of their new home, a charming stone-built manor house, constructed within a moat. The quadrangular-shaped building that Cecily and Katherine took up residence in, was, like Shute, a simple manor house. The property at Kirby had been owned by the Pakeman family during the fourteenth century and passed through inheritance to the Hastings family.[6] Later during his career, William Hastings would go on to renovate several of his Leicestershire properties as his new status allowed; he received permission for these renovations in 1474, but work did not begin on Kirby until the early 1480s so it was in the old building that Cecily would have spent a good proportion of her early childhood.

Hastings' closeness to the king quickly transformed him into a great magnate in the Midlands, and during his career he was gifted many more estates, often former Lancastrian properties. One of these land grants was at Ashby-de-la-Zouch. The last direct heir to the Zouche inheritance had died in 1399 and following several disputes over its ownership, Ashby was granted in 1462 to Lord Hastings as part of a larger grant of land in the Midlands. Hastings was acquiring immense power and wealth in the service of Edward IV which Cecily would benefit from. It is likely she visited and lived in many of these properties as she grew up.

Hastings' growing importance also enabled him to build up his household into one fit for his new wife and stepdaughter and any future children that he and Katherine would have together. His own personal retinue was vast, and his servants would travel with him around the country, providing service as well as an escort of well over one hundred men wherever he went. This peripatetic household would have included a steward, treasurer, master of the horse, grooms, kitchen clerks, master of the wardrobe, master of hounds, a carver, cooks, chaplains, and minstrels. Katherine and Cecily would also have had a smaller household that remained with them in whichever property they were residing in.

Once settled in Leicestershire, Cecily and her mother would have probably spent a fair amount of time on their own, although they were of course already accustomed to living in a female-orientated household from their time at Shute after the death of the Bonville men. Hastings, proving himself an essential part of the new Yorkist court, would have been obliged to spend a lot of time away from his Leicestershire base. Early on in Edward's reign, he was appointed Lord Chamberlain, a post that required an almost constant presence at court. The Lord Chamberlain was in effect the chief of the king's chamber and the duties were varied and important. He would have taken responsibility for ordering the king's meals, ensuring fires were lit, waking and dressing the king and running his baths – effectively he was in overall charge of running the king's chambers. With this role also came the hugely important and influential responsibility of controlling who could gain access to the king. For his service, Edward rewarded Hastings handsomely. On St George's day, 1462, he was invested as Knight of the Garter at Windsor. The Order of the Garter, created by Edward III, was of huge importance to Edward IV during his reign and it was a concept that he entirely believed in – a set of chivalrous knights, united in their friendship and loyalty. Inspired by the Legends of King Arthur, it originally consisted of 24 knights and was reserved as the highest award for loyalty and military prowess.

To be near to the court, Hastings rented a London home. The house was near Paul's Wharf (in the parish of St Benets') which he leased in June 1463 from the Austin Canons of St

Bartholomew.[7] The building was narrow but large enough for a gentleman of the court. It boasted two solars – private chambers of the Lord and Lady of the house – which were often situated on the upper floor. Here Hastings, and Katherine, if she were in London, perhaps for special occasions when her presence was required, could retire away from the hustle and bustle of the rest of the house. His London residence was within walking distance of the tower and conveniently located by the river Thames, so perfect for a gentleman often required at court.

In 1463, just over a year after their move to Leicestershire, the Neville family came together to honour their father, in a celebration which Katherine and Hastings attended together. The Earl of Salisbury had been hastily buried after his execution in 1460, and this was a chance for the family to give him a proper reburial, pay him their respects and celebrate the man he was. His wife, Countess Alice, who had died in 1461, had been buried at Bisham Priory and in 1463, the family brought her husband's body to join her there. The ceremony was followed by a great banquet at Cawood Castle. Cecily, only three or four years of age at this time, may have been considered too young to attend this reburial of her grandfather, but may have travelled with her mother and remained in the care of her nurse. Katherine and Hastings were joined in the commemorations by her brother, Warwick and her other siblings. Warwick took on the role of chief mourner.

Salisbury's cortege was escorted to the priory on Monday 14th February, where his body was received by another Neville son, Bishop George Neville. His hearse, draped in black, was carried into the choir and placed near the Countess's white covered catafalque, which was attended by the Neville women and many other gentlewomen. King Edward did not attend but he was represented by his brother George, Duke of Clarence and his sister, the Duchess of Suffolk, Salisbury's nephew and niece. The following morning, Tuesday 15th February, the mourners attended mass. After this, Warwick was formerly presented with his father's coat of arms, shield, sword helmet and crest. Hastings also took part in these formalities, presenting Warwick with the sword.[8] For Katherine and her family this must have been an occasion full of mixed emotions, mourning their father but finally being able to give him the burial they felt he deserved.

In September of the same year, Hastings and Katherine attended another Neville family celebration together, when her brother George was enthroned as Archbishop of York. The ceremony was held in York Minster, and like most medieval merriments was also followed by a great feast. A guest list of over two thousand people were served an enormous menu of oxen, sheep, pigs, deer, pike, partridges, chickens and pigeons as well as fare less familiar to us today such as swans, curlews, herons, peacocks, porpoises and seals. There were sweet dishes too in the shape of jellies, tarts and custards and the attendees also consumed three hundred tuns of ale and one hundred tun of wine. Warwick acted as steward and Hastings took the position of controller. Once again, Cecily may have been considered too young to attend. Due to the huge number of guests, several rooms were needed to accommodate all the diners, with the principal guests eating in the great hall, and in three other chambers, with the less important guests seated in the lower hall and gallery. Katherine was placed at the first table in the second chamber.[9]

With a new king on the throne, who was young, strong, and capable – an almost polar opposite of the Lancastrian Henry VI – the people of England could now hope for more peaceful and stable times ahead. For the first few years of his reign Edward concentrated on establishing himself firmly on the throne with the support of his family and friends. He was already proving himself a hugely popular king with a common touch. According to Thomas More 'he was a godly personage, and very princely to behold; of heart courageous, politic in counsel; in adversity nothing abashed, in prosperity rather joyful than proud; in peace just and merciful, in war sharp and fierce; in the field bold and hardy, and nevertheless no farther than wisdom would adventurous'.[10]

But a successful king needed a son and heir and it soon became time for the popular king to take a wife, a queen whose role it would be to provide sons to carry on the York dynasty. Having played an integral part in Edward's journey to the throne, Warwick's advice was that to secure his place there, a foreign bride would be in his best interests, bringing with her a substantial dowry and an alliance with a foreign power. To this end, Warwick was looking to France and had begun discussions for the hand of Bona of Savoy, sister of the French Queen. But in 1464 Edward made a secret marriage, to an English woman and widow named Elizabeth Woodville. Legend tells us that the wedding took place near Elizabeth's family home in Grafton Regis, on 1st May 1464, with only her mother in attendance. The marriage was kept secret for several months, until September 1464 when Edward decided to reveal the news at a meeting of the council in Reading. Warwick, seemingly unaware of this secret betrothal, was furious.

Clearly Warwick had been excluded from Edward's decision regarding his choice of bride, but it is highly probable that William Hastings was taken into Edward's confidence. Writers of historical fiction often have Hastings caught up in his master's plans, aiding his liaison with Elizabeth by accompanying him on 'hunting trips', when in truth he was making secret visits to Elizabeth's home. Although fiction, this may not be that far from what actually happened. For security reasons it would not be easy for a king to disappear off in secret without someone knowing his whereabouts, and it is highly likely that it was Hastings that assisted Edward in these clandestine meetings. Hastings himself had a connection to Elizabeth Woodville as they had once been neighbours. Her first husband was Sir John

Grey of Groby, and after her marriage Elizabeth had lived for a short while with her husband at Groby Hall, just a few miles away from Kirby Muxloe. Although the romantic story of Edward and Elizabeth's first meeting tells of Elizabeth waiting for the passing king by an oak tree, her two young sons by her side, to request the king's help with her sons' inheritance, it is not beyond the realms of possibility that it may even have been Hastings that introduced the king to his future wife.

Part of the shock of Edward's choice of new bride was the fact that Elizabeth Woodville was a widow. After the death of her first husband, who had been killed in the second battle of St Albans fighting on the Lancastrian side, Elizabeth had fallen into difficulties. From her marriage to Sir John Grey, she had borne two sons – Thomas and Richard Grey – who would have been around the ages of six and three when their father died. Elizabeth's mother-in-law, Lady Ferrers, had refused to part with what Elizabeth considered was her sons' rightful inheritance. Relations had soured to such a degree that Elizabeth had left her marital home and returned to her home at Grafton Regis. Exactly why she turned to Hastings for help is unknown, but if they knew each other as neighbours, he may have been the most powerful person she knew at the time who she felt could and would give her assistance. As it turned out, Hastings did agree to help, but it came at a price. Elizabeth had to agree to a future marriage between her son Thomas and any daughter of Hastings that was born or, if he did not father any daughters, one of his nieces. Furthermore, until Thomas was twelve years old, Hastings would have a share in any monies they could get from Lady Ferrers.[11] Elizabeth agreed and an indenture was drawn up for a marriage between Thomas Grey and any daughter born to Hastings or his brother Ralph in the next five years.

Eight months after the revelation of her marriage, Elizabeth Woodville was crowned queen. Already the mother of two sons, she had proven her fertility and the king and queen's first child together, a daughter whom they named Elizabeth, was born in 1466. Thomas and Richard Grey lived with their mother at court, and by the end of the 1460s had been joined by two more half-siblings – Mary and Cecily.

All seemed to be going well for the new royal family, but underneath the surface, trouble was brewing. Warwick had not forgiven Edward for going behind his back and it was his secret marriage to Elizabeth that many believe to have been the catalyst in the deterioration of their relationship. The Earl had created a king, but soon found he had no control over him.

As the 1460s progressed, the Earl of Warwick took against his former protégé and began 'kingmaking' once more. This time he set his sights on one of Edward's brothers – George Duke of Clarence. George was the middle brother and although seemingly handsome and charismatic, he was also selfish and indulged. Whereas their younger brother, Richard Duke of Gloucester, was as loyal to his brother as they came, George had begun to resent Edward's power. Easily led, he was quick to fall under Warwick's influence, causing a rift to form between the two brothers. In 1467, Warwick had broached the idea of a marriage between George and his eldest daughter, Isabel Neville. Perhaps sensing trouble even at this stage, Edward flatly refused to even consider the notion. But in July 1469, in direct defiance of Edward's ruling, George and Isabel travelled to Calais and were married, in a small but hugely significant ceremony.

Having gone directly against the king's wishes it was now clear that Warwick and Clarence, alongside Archbishop George Neville, were willing to openly rebel. They wrote to the king accusing members of the queen's family as well as others around the king of allowing the realm to 'fall in great poverty of misery … Only intending to their own promotion and enriching'.[12] As Clarence and Warwick returned from France, the peace that the country had enjoyed for the last few years looked to be in a fragile state.

This unpredicted turn of events must have been of some concern for Katherine Neville. Once united behind the king, she now had her brother and husband on opposing sides of a growing conflict. Hastings and Katherine by this time also had an expanding family; Cecily had been joined by a stepbrother, Edward, (most likely named after the king) who was born at Kirby Muxloe in 1465, and a further two brothers followed in the next few years, William and Richard, although their exact birth dates are unknown.[13] In 1469, Cecily would have been nine years old and able to pick up on the tension that her mother must have been feeling, if not completely understand it. As was the lot of many women during the Wars of the Roses, Katherine found herself in an impossible situation. On the one hand she had to remain loyal to her husband, whose own loyalty to his king and friend never wavered. Then on the other hand she had two of her elder brothers, Warwick and Archbishop George, now openly taking a stance against the king.

Back in England, Warwick then took what would turn out to be a doomed attempt at taking Edward prisoner. Capturing the king at Olney, near Buckingham, he took him to his home at Warwick Castle where the king remained for several weeks. Without their king, the country descended into chaos and unable to raise support for his plans to place Clarence on the throne, he embarrassingly had to let Edward go. Edward returned to London at the end of 1469 and in perhaps a naïve and foolish move, he forgave his wayward brother and cousin. But the game was not over and in March 1470 the men chose to openly rebel again. Warwick travelled to France, where he met with Henry VI's queen, Margaret of Anjou. Once bitter enemies, the pair reached an agreement that he would help restore her husband to the throne, on the condition that she agreed to a marriage between her son Edward and Warwick's youngest daughter Anne Neville. This new deal bypassed Clarence and Isabel but ensured that his second daughter would become the next queen of England. Margaret and Prince Edward had fled to France many months before where they had remained in exile, whilst old king Henry VI had been captured early on in Edward's reign and was locked up in the tower. Warwick then began preparations to sail to England with an army of men, ready to overthrow the man he had helped become king.

In the meantime, Clarence was becoming disillusioned as it became clear to him that his importance in these schemes was now waning. He was also under pressure from his family to remain loyal, particularly from his two sisters: Margaret in Burgundy and Anne back in England. Whilst still appearing to support Warwick on the surface, the Duke was 'quietly reconciled to the king by the mediation of [their] sisters, the Duchesses of Burgundy and Exeter'. The former, from outside the kingdom, had been encouraging the king, and the latter, from within, the Duke, to make peace.[14]

When Warwick landed back on England's shores, Edward was in the north of the country. Caught unawares, he found himself trapped and surrounded by rebels and unable to do anything about Warwick's army marching up from the south. The king found himself with little choice than to flee abroad himself accompanied by a small band of his most loyal men, which included his youngest brother, Richard, Duke of Gloucester and William Hastings. The group made a hasty but vital departure from England's shores in a small ship. Before they left Hastings instructed all who remained behind to make peace with Warwick for their own safety but stay loyal to Edward.[15]

The speed at which Edward's first reign was bought to an end was fast and unforeseen. Warwick arrived in London, freed Henry from the tower and for the next six months, the House of Lancaster was back in charge of the country. In a period known as the re-adaption of Henry VI, with Edward out of England, Warwick now had another chance to take the Crown under his control. Queen Elizabeth, on hearing the news and heavily pregnant, had fled into the confines of sanctuary at Westminster Abbey, taking her mother and three young daughters with her.

For the next six months, Edward, Hastings, Gloucester and their small band of supporters remained in exile. During this time, Hastings loyalty to Edward never wavered, even though he was married to the Earl of Warwick's sister. Katherine and Cecily along with her younger siblings, were left to fend for themselves in Leicestershire, undoubtedly confused and worried. Certainly, Katherine would not have felt in any danger. Her brother, Warwick, was unlikely to do her any harm, but it must still have been a stressful time, particularly if she had become close to her husband during their marriage. She must have been hugely concerned as to whether she would see him again and what would happen to him at her brother's hands if/when he did return to England. Whether Katherine had any contact with either her husband or her brother at all during these six months is unknown. It is tempting to imagine letters being sent back and forth between husband and wife, ensuring each other of their safety. Or of a distressed Katherine writing to her elder brother, demanding to know what he thought he was doing.

The exiled men were not idle during their time abroad; much of it was spent raising money and support to return. This they were able to do and six months later they sailed again for England, with Edward determined to win back his throne. Landing in the north of England, several cities not wanting trouble refused to admit him. Without an army, Edward knew he was not yet a match for his enemies and so declared himself loyal to Henry VI, and claimed he was only back in England to reclaim the York title that was rightfully his after the death of his father and brother. He began a slow march down the country, collecting men in support along the way. Hastings, meanwhile, had ridden ahead to his homelands in the Midlands and by the time Edward had reached Leicester, Hastings had gathered an army of over three thousand 'stirred by his [Hastings] messages sent unto them, and by his servants, friends and lovers, such as were in the country'.[16] We can only imagine the reunion that would have taken place when he returned to his home, his wife rejoicing in his safe return. For the twelve-year-old Cecily, Hastings was the only father she had known, so she too must also have felt relief at seeing him back safely.

Arriving back in London with an army of supporters, Edward had bypassed Warwick on his way down the country. London admitted him without question and he immediately took Henry VI back into custody before heading to Westminster sanctuary for a joyful reunion with the queen, who had given birth to a son during her time in sanctuary, naming him after his absent father. Edward now had an heir and was ready to ensure he and his family were secure on the throne once and for all.

To do this, he needed to be rid of his one-time most ardent supporter, the Earl of Warwick. A few days after arriving in London, Edward headed with his army to Barnet, ten miles outside the city where, on Easter Sunday, the two opposing armies clashed in battle. This time Hastings had a commanding role – he was on the left flank, Edward took the centre and Richard, Duke of Gloucester the right. The result was a resounding victory for the Yorkists, and in what must have been a bittersweet victory for the king, the Earl of Warwick was killed on the battlefield. Once again Katherine was to receive news of the death of one of her family members. But before Edward could finally rest safe on his throne, he had one more major battle to fight, against the Lancastrian Queen Margaret, who had landed back on the shores of England the very same day that the Battle of Barnet had been raging. With her son, Edward, by her side she was determined to defeat the Yorkist army and restore her husband, Henry VI, back to the throne of England. Upon hearing the news of her arrival, the king hurriedly raised another army and headed west from London, meeting up with the Lancastrian army at Tewkesbury where on 4th May 1471, Edward, with Hastings and Gloucester once again by his side, finally secured his throne, crushing the Lancastrians, and capturing Margaret who was brought back to London defeated and broken at the death of her son, who had been killed in the fighting. She would remain in captivity for the next four years. Shortly after, Henry VI was found dead in his rooms in the tower. It was declared he had died of natural causes, but he was most likely murdered – he was too dangerous to be kept alive, a permanent magnet for any remaining Lancastrian supporters.

The sad news of her brother's death would have filtered back to Katherine in Leicestershire. That sadness may also have been tinged with a relief that the troubles of the past few years may now finally be over and that her husband was safe and well. Throughout Hastings' prolonged absence in exile, Katherine and Cecily likely remained at Kirby or another of their Leicestershire properties, where life would have continued much as before, albeit with news of events arriving as and when it could. From this distance of time, we can never know whether Katherine's allegiances during these years lay with her brother or her husband. Most likely she would have felt herself torn between the two. But the death of her brother ensured peace would return to England and like all other women who lost relatives during these wars, she would have had to look forward and move on with her life.

Since moving to Leicestershire with Katherine at the age of two, Cecily would have been growing up in a similar vein to many young women in those times. Along with Edward, William, and Richard, Cecily was later joined by a further stepbrother, George, and two stepsisters Anne and Elizabeth, perhaps illustrating that there was a fondness or even a love between William and Katherine.[17] Cecily's early life would have revolved around the home, and she would have been fairly sheltered from external events. For young children, weaning would have been done any time between birth and the age of three and the young Cecily would have had been introduced to a week beer or ale when she was only a couple of years old. Children would also regularly drink milk, which could also be mixed with grain or flour or bread to make a gruel or porridge. Infancy ended at the age of seven, after which a child could be married or charged with a crime. From this age, boys and some girls would also have begun receiving an education. Time ruled daily life, particularly for the poor, who would get up in the light and go to bed before dark. For wealthier families who could afford candles, the setting of the sun did not affect their lives as greatly. Lives were also governed by the cyclical rotation of the year, with Saints days and festivals celebrating the turning of the seasons. Diet was also regulated to a certain extent, with the eating of meat forbidden on Fridays and around certain festivals.

Young girls like Cecily would learn much of what they needed to know from their mothers, watching and helping them with chores, such as drawing water and sweeping floors, and learning how to run a household. From the age of seven years onwards, they would learn additional tasks, such as cooking or laundry. Girls from all classes would learn sewing, spinning and weaving. Cecily may have also been taught to read by her mother, or by a tutor. In poorer households, older children would be sent out to work and as a member of a richer household, Cecily would likely have been used to young children acting as servants or pages in their house. Girls from more affluent families would work at home until they married and took charge of their own household.[18] All she learnt from her mother during these early years, would stand her in good stead when she grew up and had to manage her inherited estates and raise her own family.

Like the rest of her siblings, Cecily would have become accustomed to her stepfather's absence and perhaps she and her younger brothers and sisters would have waited in anticipation when they knew he was due home, excitedly listening for the sound of hooves heralding his return. As well as his extended exile abroad, from the 1470s onwards, his absence from home may have been for even longer periods of time, for as well as his court duties, he now had to spend time in France.

Hastings had well and truly proved his loyalty to his king throughout the six long months abroad and in the ensuing battles upon their return at Barnet and Tewkesbury and for that loyalty, he was once again handsomely rewarded. As well as being made constable of Nottingham castle, he was also awarded the position of Lieutenant of Calais – his official title being 'Guard-General, Superintendent, Governor, and Lieutenant of the king at Calais at the castle and town'. This was a hugely important post. Whoever held the role of Lieutenant (or Captain) of Calais was in effect the king's deputy. He ruled over all inhabitants and visitors to the town and was required to maintain law and order in the garrison and keep the town and its residents safe. A deputy was also in post who would resume command in the absence of the Lieutenant. This new position would have kept him away from Katherine and the children for lengthy periods of time and for the next few years he would have to become accustomed to spending considerable amounts of time on horseback or aboard a ship as he journeyed between Leicestershire, the court and the continent.

Since Henry VI had lost all the remaining French lands that his father had won back, the pale of Calais was now the last English outpost in France. Calais was the medieval equivalent of English Gibraltar as it is today, an English outpost situated on the tip of the Spanish mainland. Hastings already owned property there as in 1465 he had received an inn called Nettelbedd with two tenements in St Nicholas as a gift from his uncle Lord

Camoys.[20] Therefore, arriving in Calais in his role of Lieutenant, he may already have been familiar with the town.

What Hastings was like as a stepfather, or even as a husband we can only guess at. Were Katherine and Cecily happy to have him home on the occasions he could return to them or did they fare just as well in his absence? Hastings certainly had a reputation as a notorious philanderer, as did his king, and he had plenty of opportunity spending so much time away. But he also had the reputation of being an honourable and likeable man. Described by Thomas More as '[an] honourable man, a good knight and a gentle, of good authority with his prince'. More tells us he possessed 'a good heart and courage … a loving man and passing well beloved; very faithful, and trusty enough, trusting too much'. If he was genuinely as kind and loving to his family as he was to his king, then he most likely proved himself a good stepfather to Cecily.

That their relationship was a close one is perhaps illustrated by the fact that when Cecily was around thirteen years of age, she went to visit her stepfather in Calais, in what must have been an exciting trip for the young teenager. This occasion, which took place around April 1473, was reported in a letter from John Paston who wrote from Dover on 16th April 1473 that Hastings had sent for his stepdaughter along with a daughter of Sir Thomas Hungerford and his young neighbour from the Midlands, Lord Zouche, describing them as three great jewels. John Paston pre-empted that the trip would be enjoyable to them, reporting that 'Calais is a merry town'.[21]

Item, my Lorde Chamberleyn sendyth now at thys tyme to Caleys the yonge Lorde Sowche and Sir Thomas Hongreffords dowtre and heyr and some seye the yonge Lady Haryngton, thes be iij. grett jowelles, Caleys is a mery town, they shall dwell ther I wott not whylghe [how long].

How long they did remain went unrecorded, but it must have been with huge excitement and trepidation that Cecily waited on the English coast, ready to board the ship for France. This was very possibly her first trip abroad. The 'merry town' of Calais was filled with merchants and soldiers as these were the main trades of the town – the garrison served to protect the merchants of the town. The pale of Calais, which covered an area of roughly twenty square miles, was divided into the high country on the west and the low country on the east. The higher parts were comprised of tiny villages nestling in small valleys whilst the lower parts consisted of marshier ground, necessitating the upkeep of ditches and banks. In the main town there were several churches as well as the Staple Hall and the Town Hall, the Castle and the main Square of St Nicholas. Criss-crossing their way across the town was no less than forty-one streets, with recognisably English names such as Cow Lane, Rigging Street and Duke Street.[22]

Back home in England, Hastings was further rewarded for his service and loyalty in April 1474, when King Edward granted him licence to make improvements to some of his properties, which included permission to crenellate. Crenellating the house meant the owner had permission to add battlements. As this then fortified the property, permission had to be sought first from the Crown. At the same time, he also received a licence to enclose off land around his properties for hunting. At Ashby, he turned 3000 acres of land and wood into parkland, 2000 more at Kirby and another 2000 acres at two other properties he owned in Bagwell and Thornton. He was also given permission to erect fortified houses of lime and stone in these manors. Up until then, Kirby Muxloe had always been their primary residence, but from the mid-1470s, it seems that Hastings' plans perhaps involved turning the manor at Ashby into the family's main home. The first reference to work there is in the manorial roll for 1472–3, which refers to 'diverse great works within the manor and the wages of carpenters, tillers, masons, plumbers and other artificers and their servants' and reveals that work was begun before he received his licence to crenellate.[23]

The castle at Ashby was on the south side of the town, on elevated ground and surrounded by three great parks: Great Park which was the largest, Preston Park which was brimming with fallow deer and Little Park to the rear of the house full of red deer. The original property Hastings had received at Ashby had once been a Norman manor house, likely constructed of timber. This had been replaced by previous owners by a more substantial stone building sometime in the latter half of the twelfth century. By the mid-fourteenth century the main building was described as 'a capital messuage worth nothing' and containing a 'ruinouse old hall'.[24] When Hastings took ownership of the property, it already featured two towers, built of Ashler stone, on the south and south west side. His ambitious plans involved constructing two more so that the end result would have been four great towers set around a perimeter wall. Work began on the existing manor house and Hastings had it extensively remodelled and expanded with a new chapel. The greater of the two existing towers was almost an entire house in itself consisting of large hall, great chambers, bed chambers, a kitchen, a cellar, and numerous other offices. The other tower, known as the kitchen tower, contained an entire kitchen which was one of the largest of its kind. Above this huge kitchen were many more fine rooms.[25] If completed, the castle would have been magnificent. As it was, by the time of his death only half of his plans had come to fruition. In years to come the castle at Ashby would find fame for being the temporary prison of Mary Queen of Scots. Hastings' grand house at Ashby is now in ruins, today in the care of English Heritage, but visitors can still get a sense of the grandeur of the building.

Although Ashby was likely intended to become his primary residence, Hastings did not forget Kirby, although as mentioned previously, work did not begin there until the early 1480s when he was at the pinnacle of his career; his massive wealth by that time is reflected in the building works. His plans at Kirby were for a modern residence, centred around a courtyard and surrounded by a wide moat. The buildings were constructed from the local red brick, with stone used for details such as windows and doors – a combination that in those times was the height of fashion. The castle was to be oblong shaped with angle towers, an enormous gatehouse and ranges of buildings set round an inner courtyard. Four masons were hired to create 'pictures in the walls' using darker bricks; in the gatehouse these included the initials WH, the sleeve from Hastings's coat of arms, a ship and a jug.

When Hastings died in mid-1483, work was in progress at Kirby and the bricklayers, masons and carpenters all stopped work immediately. They resumed construction later in the year but on a much smaller scale and by September 1484 work had stopped completely, with much of the castle remaining unfinished. Once again today the ruins at Kirby are under the care of English Heritage and the gatehouse and one of the corner towers survive within the moated site, offering a glimpse of what Hastings had intended to be one of the most advanced and fashionable manor houses of its time.

The year after Cecily's visit to Calais, her family began planning for her marriage. Her intended husband was none other than Thomas Grey, son of Queen Elizabeth. After Elizabeth became queen, her agreement with Hastings was broken off and instead a marriage had been arranged between Thomas and Anne Holland, the daughter of Anne of York, Edward IV's sister. The marriage between Thomas and Anne took place in Greenwich in 1466 when Anne was around five years old and Thomas aged around twelve.

Cecily had also initially been promised to someone else – her cousin, George Neville, son of the Marquis of Montagu, who in a curious set of circumstances had been previously betrothed to Thomas' new bride, Anne Holland. Cecily's match with George had never been finalised and when Anne Holland died in 1474, a match was proposed between Thomas and Cecily. Queen Elizabeth agreed to pay Hastings 2500 marks for the marriage and an agreement was reached that the queen would receive income from all of Cecily's estates until she reached sixteen years of age and controversially that if the couple were childless upon Thomas' death, her inheritance would go to Richard Grey (Thomas' brother) and not any of Cecily's heirs that she may have had from a second marriage. What Cecily would have thought about this we can only imagine, but nevertheless she would have had no choice in the matter. Presumably if she dwelt on it at all, she would have had to put it to the back of her mind and look forward to the next stage of her life, as a married woman and daughter-in-law of the Queen of England. It was now time for a new chapter in Cecily's life, as a wife, mother and Marchioness.

Chapter Three

The Wife of Thomas Grey

1474-1483

As the stepdaughter of the Lord Chamberlain, Cecily would have been no stranger to court life. No doubt Hastings regaled them with tales of the goings-on at court during his visits home and Cecily may even have visited along with her mother when the occasion arose, perhaps for the Christmas festivities or to attend the christenings of the royal children. The king and queen had ten children together between the years of 1466 and 1480. But now that that she was the wife of the king's stepson, Cecily was moving even closer to the inner circles of the royal family. Her marriage contract to Thomas Grey was dated 18 July 1474 and their required dispensation (due to their joint descendance from one Reginald Grey), was received 5th September 1474.[1] Their wedding ceremony would certainly have befitted that of the stepson of the king and no doubt both the king and queen would have attended this lavish affair. After the nuptials, Cecily would have said goodbye to her homes at Kirby and Ashby and the other Hastings properties she had resided in, as well as a fond farewell to her mother and gone to join her husband, possibly in rooms at court initially; she was fourteen or fifteen and he was around the age of nineteen.

Cecily's grandmother, Elizabeth Bonville, whom she had been so close to as a child, had died three years previously in 1471 so had not lived to see the young girl she was so fond of reach a marriageable age. At the time of her marriage Cecily was still not quite old enough to inherit her childhood home; that would come to her just under a year later when on 12th April 1475, she was finally in receipt of her family estates. This may point to an actual birth date of around early 1459 for Cecily as she would have been sixteen when she received her inheritance. Eleven days later Thomas and Cecily received licence to enter her lands. It was now time for them to make a home for themselves and any children they may have together.[2]

1475 was to be a busy year for the couple and this was also the year that Thomas received the title that he would become synonymous with throughout history. Upon surrendering his earlier title of Earl of Huntingdon which he had been awarded on 14th August 1471, he was given a far greater honour when on 18th April 1475 the king bestowed upon him the title of Marquis of Dorset. Cecily as his wife would now become the Marchioness of Dorset.[3]

This honour perhaps illustrates that a real fondness existed between the king and his stepson. As Marquis, he now took precedence over most of the court; the title of Marquis being just one step down from Duke, and there were only seven Dukes in existence at that time, including the king's two brothers: George, Duke of Clarence and Richard, Duke of Gloucester. As well as a new title, Thomas also received a knighthood alongside his brother, Richard Grey and his uncle, Edward Woodville. All three were made Knights of the Bath in honour of the young Prince Edward, during his investiture as Prince of Wales. Two weeks after this Thomas, or Dorset as he would become known, was also admitted to Edward's precious Order of the Garter.[4]

Prince Edward, as the new Prince of Wales and heir to the throne, was sent to reside at Ludlow Castle, in the Welsh Marshes, a property owned by the Crown and away from the bustle and dangers of London. He was established here in his own household that aimed to prepare him for future kingship, and both Dorset and his brother Richard were known to have spent some of their time there with him. As his wife, Cecily may also have paid a visit to this imposing castle with her husband. Built on a rocky outcrop overlooking the river Teme, Ludlow

Castle would also become the home of future heirs to the throne and in the next generation would house the young Arthur Tudor and his new bride Katherine of Aragon, before Arthur's tragic death.

The spring of 1475 was also the chosen year for a new French campaign. King Edward, following in the footsteps of kings who had come before him, raised an army to cross the channel to invade France, their aim once again to conquer and reclaim French lands. On 1st of May a proclamation was made requesting 'all the lordes and capitaignes' to muster at Portsdown in the county of Southampton. Towards the end of the month, on the 26th May, John Lord Dynham, by letters patent dated the 15th of April, was appointed to conduct the army across the sea. The king had left London on the 4th of May and proceeded towards the coast through the county of Kent. On the 6th and 10th he was at Canterbury, and on the 20th at Sandwich, where on that day he made his Will. After a small delay, the king and his army crossed the channel on the 4th of July. In his retinue, amongst others, were his two brothers, the Dukes of Clarence and Gloucester, William Hastings and Dorset.

Upon landing at Calais, the king was met by his sister the Duchess of Burgundy and her husband, the Duke. Margaret had left England after her marriage to the Duke of Burgundy in 1468. The party travelled together to the castle of Guisnes and spent some time together there. The aim of the French trip had been war, but much to the disappointment of some of his army who had been geared up to fight, the expedition did not go quite as planned. Instead of being the conquering force they had set out to be, Edward accepted a pay-off from his French counterpart, King Louis. The treaty between Louis and Edward was concluded on the 13th of August whilst Edward and his men were camped out 'in his felde beside a village called Seyntre, within Vermondose, a litell from Peronne'.[5] 16,000 crowns were made available to be offered in pensions to some of those in attendance, and Hastings certainly benefitted, being promised 2000 crowns a-year. Many of the other men also received money and plate that was distributed among the rest of the king's retinue and Dorset was also no doubt one of those financially rewarded. Louis and Edward agreed that the truce would last for nine years and upon his departure Edward agreed to leave behind a few of his men as 'hostages', to be released once he had returned to England's shores. The king and his men returned to England somewhat richer, but some, including the king's younger brother, Gloucester, were disappointed not to be returning as the victors they had set out to be.

Left behind in England while her new husband travelled to France with the king, Cecily was forming grand plans to renovate her beloved old manor at Shute and make it into a home for her and her family. It may have been whilst Dorset was on campaign in France that she first travelled back to her childhood home, with plans for him to join her on his return. It is possible that she visited there during her younger years to visit Elizabeth, but it must have been with a great excitement and an optimism for the future that she made her first journey back as the Lady of the Manor. Despite the fact that she had suffered such family losses here as a young child, and that she had left it as a toddler, it clearly illustrates her genuine connection to Devon and Shute in particular. She held a real affection for her place of birth and it was to here she chose to return and start her family.

The manor house at Shute where Cecily had been born had lost none of its appeal and as she approached for the first time as its owner, Cecily cannot have failed to appreciate its beauty. Leland, recording in his itinerary in the sixteenth century, wrote of Shute: 'I saw from an hille Shoute, a right goodly maner place, a mile of on an hille side of the Lorde Marquise of Dorsete, and by it a goodly large park'.[6]

Now that she had come into her inheritance, Cecily and

Dorset were now vast landowners. An inventory of her lands taken in 1525 by Richard Phellyps, her surveyor, of her properties in Devon, Cornwall, Somerset, Dorset and Wiltshire records 79 'manors', some of which were tenements or plots of land, comprising around 30,000 acres and with a rental amount of £1000, which equates to approximately £700,000 in today's currency. She also owned property in several other counties as well as in London as part of her huge legacy. Much of this property was rented out but some would have been available for Cecily and Dorset to occupy[7], including the nearby Wiscombe Park in Devon, which would become another of their favoured properties. But seemingly it was Shute that they wished to make their primary residence, although the couple would and did travel backwards and forwards to court and between their other houses. Medieval households of the richer classes were much more peripatetic than in later periods, and when leaving one property for another, all their household goods would be loaded up onto carts, with children and servants riding on horseback or carried in litters. This afforded families the luxury of being able to travel around the country and also allowed thorough cleaning of the properties whilst the Lord and Lady were absent.

By 1476, Cecily had certainly returned to court to witness her husband take part in the annual St George's day ceremony at Windsor. On the day of the ceremony, which was a Sunday, the king and his knights rode together to Matins, before breakfasting together with the Dean, Bishop Beauchamp. Later they attended High Mass together. Cecily was present at the ceremony to watch her husband take his position as a new Garter knight, alongside the king and queen, and their eldest daughter – the Princess Elizabeth. Also present amongst the ladies was the Duchess of Suffolk (the king's sister) and Anne Hastings. The ladies gathered to watch the proceedings from seats in the rood loft.[8] The following day the king and knights went in procession to the chapter house and the choir where each stood in front of his stool.

Another significant event in the life of the royal family also took place that year when King Edward and his brothers arranged the reburial of Edward's father, the Duke of York. As the Nevilles had done some thirteen years previous with the Earl of Salisbury, Edward and his brothers wanted to lay their father to rest with the dignity he deserved. Firmly now established on his throne, Edward was able to give the matter his full attention and threw his finances into this act of honouring his father and brother, Edmund, Earl of Rutland, who had been killed alongside his father. Both has been hastily buried in Pontefract after their deaths at the battle of Wakefield and the family wanted to bring their bodies home to the family mausoleum at Fotheringhay. This hugely personal and important event to the king and his family took place in July of that year, when Edward's younger brother, Gloucester, arrived in Pontefract to escort the cortege from St John's priory on its journey south to its final resting place. The coffins, covered in rich palls of cloth-of-gold, were placed upon carriages pulled by teams of black horses. Accompanying the solemn procession were four hundred 'poor men' carrying torches, their black hoods up over their heads. All along the route nightly vigils were held at each pre-arranged resting place.

The cortege arrived at the churchyard in Fotheringhay at midday on 29th July, to be greeted by Edward dressed in a blue robe, the royal colour of mourning, flanked by his two brothers, Clarence and Gloucester, the latter who had ridden ahead for the last part of the journey so he could be there with his brothers to meet the procession. Many of their closest friends and family were present to repay their respects. Dorset certainly was and it is likely that Cecily may very well have been there with him. The funeral service was held the following day, followed by a lavish feast where up to two thousand guests dined in canvas pavilions erected especially for the occasion in neighbouring fields.[9]

Perhaps then returning to Shute manor, Cecily and Dorset began their extensive alterations to the manor house. Rather than change the existing building, the couple planned to build a new mansion house onto the north side of the old manor. This task would take them several years and their new extension included, amongst other things, an oratory, and a beautifully designed solar with mullioned windows overlooking formal gardens and the Devonshire countryside to the south-east. The solar offered the utmost privacy, with the only entrance into the room from a hexagonal old turret. This solar would become the private apartment for the Dorsets when they were in residence.

A year later, in 1477, Cecily gave birth to a son whom they named Thomas after his father. He was born at Shute in 1477 and his birth was considered notable enough to be mentioned by John Paston in a letter written on 23rd June 1477: 'Tydyngs butt that yisterdaye my Lady Marqueys off Dorset, whych is my Lady Hastyngs dowtr, hadyd chylde a sone'.[10]

Things seemed to be going well for the young married couple. The birth of a son and heir would have been an occasion for celebration, and they would have had great optimism for more sons to follow. The troubles in England also seemed to be fading into the past. By the mid-1470s, the wars of the 1460s and the temporary hiatus in Edward's reign in early 1470/1 were disappearing into the annals of history. By 1477 Edward was now seemingly secure on the throne of England and the king and queen also had a growing family, providing Dorset with five half-sisters, Elizabeth, Mary, Cecily, Margaret and Anne and two half-brothers, Edward and Richard.

With Warwick dead, Edward's wayward brother Clarence had come back into the fold. Settling into family life with his wife, Isabel, they now had two young children and he spent more of his time away from court and with his young family.

The brother's show of unity at the reburial of their father portrayed a sign of harmony – that all was well. But behind the scenes trouble was once again looming. In late 1476 Clarence's wife, Isabel, died shortly after giving birth. The grieving Duke, looking for someone to blame, cited witchcraft, accusing one of his wife's servants, Ankarette Twynyho of poisoning his wife. Much to the horror of her family, Clarence had her arrested and summarily executed immediately after a trial, during which he heavily influenced the jurors to pronounce a guilty verdict. Her family complained to the king and Edward once again attempted to reel in his unruly brother.

But Clarence's destructive behaviour only accelerated. In a move perhaps designed to antagonise the king, Clarence began to seek a new wife; his bride of choice was Mary of Burgundy, the stepdaughter of his sister, Margaret. Edward once again refused to allow his brother to get his way and Clarence received the news with ill grace and left court, refusing to dine with the king and queen, whilst making bizarre accusations that the queen's family were trying to poison him.

The disruptive chain of events continued when three men were arrested, accused of plotting Edward's death. One of the accused was a close associate of Clarence, and all three were found guilty at trial, with two out of the three being executed for treason. This should have been a warning to Clarence, but he ignored it. Instead, he aligned himself with a notorious Lancastrian preacher and burst into Parliament to protest the innocence of the condemned men, whilst at the same time taking verbal pot-shots at the king and disrespecting the queen and her family. Edward could not let this continue and in the summer of 1477 found himself with little choice but to arrest his troublesome brother.

Clarence was put on trial for treason and Edward elected to personally question his brother. With the two pitted against each other the Croyland Chronicle reported that 'no one spoke against the Duke but the king, and no one answered but the Duke'. Clarence was convicted and despite desperate pleas for clemency by their mother, on 18th February 1478, George Duke of Clarence, was put to death in the most infamous of executions, reportedly having been given the freedom of choosing his own manner of death, he elected to be drowned in a barrel of Malmsey wine.

These were dramatic events as they played out and although the king perhaps had little choice in the actions he took, it was an ugly chapter in his reign and one that undeniably must have caused waves between the king's relatives and friends. Their younger brother, Richard of Gloucester, one of, if not the most loyal supporters of the king was said to be hugely upset at this turn of events and appeared less at court in the following months and years. Dorset, however, did well out of Clarence's death. He received stewardships that had once belonged to Clarence and two years later, in 1480, he was granted the wardship and marriage of the Duke's son, Edward, the new young Earl of Warwick, for which he paid £2000. This allowed him to profit from the Earl's lands until he came of age. If the Earl died, Dorset would also be guaranteed the wardship and marriage of Margaret, Clarence and Isabel's daughter, who would have inherited the Warwick estates upon the death of her brother.

The young Earl of Warwick would have been taken to live with the Dorsets and during the next few years, their own family would also grow. No exact birth dates have been recorded for their children, but by the time of the young Earl of Warwick's arrival in 1480, they had likely had their second son, another boy whom they named Richard (perhaps as a tribute to Richard Grey, Dorset's brother). Occupied with the renovations at Shute, and two young children in the nursery and a young ward to look after, Cecily and Dorset had their hands full.

In late 1477, early 1478, Dorset had once again returned to London for the wedding of his young half-brother, Richard, the king and queen's second son, to Anne Mowbray, the only daughter of John Duke of Norfolk. The young prince was just four years old and his bride to be only five or six. Like Cecily, Anne Mowbray was the sole heiress of a vast inheritance that came to her upon the death of her father. The marriage took place on Thursday 15th January 1478 in Saint Stephen's chapel, in the palace of Westminster. The occasion was another cause for celebration for the royal family and the festivities had been weeks in the planning.

On 10th December 1477, a few weeks before the wedding, a proclamation had been made by six gentleman challengers, announcing a grand joust to follow the wedding celebrations. The announcements detailing the jousts were placed in three spots around London, the first, at the gate of the King's Palace (presumably Westminster), the second in Cheapside and the third upon London Bridge. Amongst the challengers were Dorset, his brother Richard Grey and Sir Edward Woodville (the queen's brother).

The wedding rehearsals took place on the 14th January in the king's chamber at Westminster, in the presence of 'many great estates and degrees, Dukes and earles, and barons, and with great abundance of ladies and gentlewomen'.[11] Cecily may well have been part of this group of ladies. The following day, 15th January, Anne was led out of the queen's chamber at Westminster, through the king's great chamber and into the White Hall, before entering St Stephen's chapel. The chapel had been richly decorated for the occasion and under a canopy made of cloth of gold, the king, the queen, and the little prince stood waiting to receive her. Also waiting there was the king's mother and the three eldest York Princesses – Elizabeth, Mary and Cecily. The service was conducted by the Bishop of Norwich and the ceremony was followed by spices and wine, as was the custom.

After the ceremony, the wedding party proceeded to the

grand feast, which was attended by the Duchess of Norfolk, Anne's mother, and many other members of the nobility. Dorset was seated at the first side table, and presumably Cecily was with him, although not necessarily seated by him. So many people had been invited to the celebrations that the recorder of the event wrote that the 'presse was soe great that I might not see to write the names of them that served; the abundance of the noble people were so innumerable'.[12]

A week later, the planned jousts in celebration of the newly married couple took place at Westminster. Dorset was the first to enter the lists, although the grandest entrance was made by Anthony, Earl Rivers, the queen's brother, who appeared in the house of a Hermit, which was walled and covered with black velvet. In stark contrast, the Earl was appropriately dressed in the habit of a White Hermit. As he exited the hermitage, his servants pulled the habit from him as rehearsed and he proceeded on his horse to enter the tournaments. Dorset it seems was evenly matched in the jousting against Sir William Trussell, with both parties breaking two spears each out of their six courses.

Spectators of the jousts included the king and queen and their children, as well as many other Dukes, earls, ladies and gentlewomen. The Ambassadors of France, Scotland, Burgoyne, and Almaine were also in attendance. Cecily once again was highly likely to have been one of the ladies. Once the jousting had ending, Anne Mowbray, the Princess of the feast withdrew 'with all estates of ladyes and gentlewomen, to the king's great chamber in Westminster, where there her Minstrells, and all ladyes, and gentlewomen, lords, knights, and esquires, to dancinge; and soe passed the tyme for a space'.[13]

Cecily and Dorset were back at court once again in 1480 at the christening of what was, unbeknownst to them, the king and queen's last child. Princess Bridget was born on 10th November

1480 at the palace of Eltham and the christening was held the next day. As was the custom the king and queen did not attend the christening, so it was left to family members to accompany the new-born to her first official engagement. Dorset, as the new infant's half-brother, assisted the Countess of Richmond, Margaret Beaufort, in carrying the Princess into the chapel. Her paternal grandmother, Cecily Neville and Bridget's eldest sister, fourteen-year-old Elizabeth of York, were godmothers at the baptismal font and one of the queen's sisters, Margaret (Lady Maltravers), was also honoured as godmother to the confirmation.

In the twentieth year of the reign of King Edward IV on St. Martin's Eve was born the Lady Bridget, and christened on the morning of St. Martin's Day in the Chapel of Eltham, by the Bishop of Chichester in order as ensueth:

First a hundred torches borne by knights, esquires, and other honest persons.

The Lord Maltravers, bearing the basin, having a towel about his neck.

The Earl of Northumberland bearing a taper not lit.

The Earl of Lincoln the salt.

The canopy borne by three knights and a baron.

My lady Maltravers did bear a rich crysom pinned over her left breast.

The Countess of Richmond did bear the princess.

My lord Marquess Dorset assisted her.

My lady the king's mother, and my lady Elizabeth, were godmothers at the font.

And when the said princess was christened, a squire held the basins to the gossips [the godmothers], and even by the font my Lady Maltravers was godmother to the confirmation.

Cecily Dorset would almost certainly have been there alongside her husband, unless of course she too was in confinement around this time. Their sons, Thomas and Richard, were followed by another brother, John and their first daughter, Eleanor, who were both born sometime before 1481. As well as the ever-expanding nursery, the Dorset household would also have consisted of around 50-100 servants including Cecily's lady attendants, the children's nurses, a chaplain, and stewards. Another young ward had also joined the household by this point, a young girl named Joan Durnford. Joan was the heiress of the Durnford family, a powerful Devon family who owned vast amounts of land around Plymouth and Stonehouse, and who would in her later years marry Sir Piers Edgecumbe in 1493, joining her fortunes with that of the large Edgecumbe estates. [14]

Although Dorset was riding high in the esteem of the king and the couple were very much part of court life, little is heard directly of Cecily in the few years after her marriage. Presumably, she spent much of her time at Shute, supervising the renovations and raising her ever-growing family. We can, however, catch a glimpse of Cecily in the spring of 1482 when she spent some time with her cousin Anne at Taunton.

Her cousin Anne was the daughter of John Neville, the Marquis of Montagu and the third wife of Sir William Stonor. Letters detailing the life and activities of the Stonor family up to 1483 (at which date Sir John was attainted and his papers seized and held by the crown) are still extant today and held in the National Archives. They offer an intriguing glimpse into life in the 13th to 15th centuries.

Anne was newly married to William, when on 27th February 1482 she wrote to him from Taunton.

Syr, I recomaund me unto you in my most h[ert]y wise, right joyfull to here of yowre helthe: liketh you to knowe, at þe writyng of þis bill I was in good helthe, thynkyng long sith I saw you, and if I had knowen þat I shold hav ben this long tyme from you I wold have be moche lother then I was to have comyn into this ferre Countrey. But I trust it shall not be long or I shall see you here, and else I wold be sorye on good feith. Syr, I am moche byholdyng to my lady, for she maketh right moche of me, and to all the company, officers and other. I have early trust uppon your comyng unto þe tyme of thassise, and else I wold have send Herry Tye to you long or þis tyme. I have delyvered a bill to Herry Tye of suche gownes as I wold have for þis Ester. And I beseche oure blessed lord preserve you. From the Castell of Taunton þe xxvij day of Februarer.

Your new wyf Anne Stonor[15]

The 'my lady' she refers to is Cecily and the two women were in each other's company at Taunton Castle, a residence that was part of Cecily's inheritance. The castle had been originally built by William Giffard, Bishop of Winchester in the 12th century and Lord William Bonville had been besieged in his castle of Taunton in 1449 by the Earl of Devon. The manor and castle of Taunton came to his widow Elizabeth after his death and therefore formed part of Cecily's inheritance.[16]

Later in May the two ladies moved on to Dartington Castle. On 15th May, just before the ladies were set to depart, a Stonor family servant, John Payne, wrote to his master, informing him the women were now leaving for Dartington 'for my lady and all the household shall hastily to Dartington, and here remain a season'. He signs the letter 'One of your servants, John Payne, with My Lord Marquis', so it seems Dorset may well have been with the ladies at the time.

The manor of Dartington, where the ladies were hastily departing to, belonged to the Crown. Gifted by King Richard II to his half-brother, John Holland Duke of Exeter, who resided at Dartington and is said to have built most of the mansion and the great hall. It passed down through the family to Henry

Holland, 3rd Duke of Exeter, who married the king's sister, Anne of York. Exeter hated his father-in-law the Duke of York and his marriage was an unhappy one. He sided with the Lancastrians during the troubles, fleeing into exile with Margaret of Anjou. Anne of York divorced him, and he was attainted by Edward IV, with the manor reverting to the crown.[17]

From these letters we can see that even after her marriage into the royal circles, Cecily still maintained relationships with her mother's side of the family. Cecily may well have been pregnant during some of this time period as following on from Eleanor's birth which may even have fallen in 1482, a fourth son, Anthony, had joined their ever-growing brood by 1483. Cecily would have been living the life of a typical high-born lady of her time. With fairly regular pregnancies, perhaps we can read into that that she enjoyed a close relationship with her husband and with hope and optimism for the future, and a broader peace in the land, life was seemingly going well. But then in 1483 everything changed, when King Edward died, and the country was once again thrown into turmoil.

Chapter Four

The Reign of Richard III

1483-1485

In March 1483, King Edward had been at Windsor. In his *Itinerary of Edward IV*, John Ashdown Hill places Edward at Windsor from Tuesday 4th March, returning to Westminster just before Easter Sunday around Tuesday 25th March. Upon his return to London, he was taken so violently ill that he retired to his sickbed. What the illness was that eventually led to his death was a matter of speculation even then and remains so today. Dominic Mancini, an Italian poet who spent some time in England during early 1483 and recorded what he witnessed upon his return to his homeland later that year, believed that the king had caught a cold from a recent fishing trip. His death was also attributed by other sources at the time to an ague or fever or even a stroke. What we do know is that in the days before his death, he was in a state of consciousness and during that time he added several codicils to his Will. One of those codicils was allegedly designed to heal a rift that had grown between his stepson Dorset, and best friend, Hastings. Calling the men to his bedside he pleaded with them to put aside their differences. Then on 9th April, Edward died. He was not yet forty-one and his son, Edward Prince of Wales, was just twelve. Presumably, Edward was well aware that at such a young age his son, now King Edward V, would need his close family and friends around him and would need the support of both of these men to ensure a smooth transition of power and to guide his young son in the early months and years of his kingship.

But what was this rift that had occurred between Dorset and his father-in-law Hastings? Thomas More tells us in his description of Edward's last few days 'but in his last sickness when he perceived his natural strength so sore enfeebled that he despaired all recovery... he called some of them before him that were at variance, and in especial the Lord Marquis Dorset, the queen's son by her first husband, and Richard [William] the Lord Hastings, a nobleman then lord chamberlain, again whom the queen specially grudged for the great favor the king bare him and also for that she thought him secretly familiar with the king in wanton company'. More goes on to say that the king begged them [Dorset and Hastings] to reconcile 'for all the love that you have ever borne to me, for the love that I have ever borne to you' and that 'amongst much weeping they joined hands and forgave each other'.[1]

The common view of the enmity between Dorset and Hastings centres around the promiscuous behaviour of either one or both of these men, and in particular their love or infatuation towards a particular lady named Jane Shore. Jane Shore had been one of Edward IV's mistresses. Famously he was known to have at least three, whom he allegedly categorised as 'the merriest, the wiliest and the holiest' women in the land. Jane is believed to have been the 'merriest'. Born Elizabeth Lambert sometime around 1450, she was the daughter of a mercer, John Lambert and his wife Amy. Her marriage to another mercer, one William Shore, occurred sometime in the mid-to-late 1460s but within a few years she appealed to the court of Arches, requesting a divorce and alleging that her marriage was unconsummated. This in itself was a courageous move for her to make, as women rarely initiated separation from their husbands. The appeal was denied, but Jane demonstrating a huge amount of tenacity refused to give up. She took the matter to court more than once and was eventually granted a divorce on 1st March 1476, around about the same time she is thought to have become the king's mistress. How she met the king is unclear. Whether he assisted her in her divorce matter also went unrecorded, but it is not beyond the realms of possibility that the two were linked.[2]

Although it appears that in the early days Hastings and Elizabeth Woodville were on good terms, it seems that by the time of Edward's death the queen no longer had a high regard for her husband's best friend as over the years he was apparently often found with Edward in pursuit of 'wanton company'. Perhaps she turned more of a blind eye to the actions of her son, assuming he also partook in these clandestine liaisons. Mancini describes the ongoing conflict between Hastings and Dorset as a jealousy – 'as a result of the mistresses they had abducted or attempted to entice from each other'.

With reference to Jane Shore in particular, according to More 'when the king died, the Lord Chamberlain took her – which in the king's days, albeit he was sore enamored upon her, yet he forbare her, either for reverence or for a certain friendly faithfulness'. If this is true, Hastings may not have had a sexual relationship with Jane Shore during the king's lifetime. Perhaps even after Edward's death he was just extremely fond of the young woman and wished to protect her. It is often alleged however, particularly during the events that followed, that Dorset did have a relationship with her. In which case their arguments may have centred around the fact that Hastings had knowledge of this relationship and was either jealous, as Mancini alleges, or perhaps he was aggrieved on behalf of his stepdaughter, Cecily. But, of course, the reverse could also be true; if Hastings had been Jane Shore's lover, perhaps Dorset was aggrieved on Cecily's behalf, as she, quite rightly, would have been upset on behalf of her mother, Katherine. Or perhaps it was that in the licentious court of Edward IV, both men were vying for her affection and that as Mancini alleges, they delighted in stealing or enticing her away from each other.

But for now, they had, it seemed, agreed to put their differences aside and support Edward's young son. Edward IV's funeral took place ten days after his death, on Friday 19th April.

On Wednesday 17th April, the king's body had been conveyed to Westminster Abbey from St Stephen's chapel where he had lain since his passing. The coffin was draped with a pall of cloth of gold with a cross of white cloth of gold. Within forty-eight hours of the king's death, letters were sent across the country proclaiming Edward V the new king and announcing a coronation date of 4th May. The young prince had been written to in Ludlow and summoned to return to London, but he was not expected to arrive in time for the funeral. Reportedly Hastings himself wrote to inform the king's brother, Richard of Gloucester, who was at his home in the north, but he also did not arrive in time to see his brother laid to rest. Who took the place of chief mourner has not been identified but the first of those present in the line of precedence was the king's eldest nephew, the Earl of Lincoln, son of Edward's sister Elizabeth. It was presumably he who acted as chief mourner and would have walked directly behind the coffin in its procession from St Stephens to the Abbey.[3] Also in the procession were Hastings and Dorset. Cecily would not have attended as a king's funeral was primarily a male affair.

After a service in the Abbey, the coffin was loaded upon a chariot for Edward's last journey to Windsor. Six horses were ready to pull the chariot, each in trappings of black velvet. Two chariot men sat on the front two horses, while four of the king's henchmen, whose names went unrecorded, rode the other four. The procession then set off on its way, spending the night of the 17th at Syon Abbey where the Bishop of Durham conducted a late service, as the cortege did not arrive until after dark.

The following day, Thursday 18th April, the procession set off again, arriving at Windsor later that day. Edward's final destination was St George's chapel, the place he had been rebuilding since the early 1470s as his family mausoleum. It was also designed to be a chapel for his beloved Order of the Garter. By the time of his burial there, it was not yet finished but it was roofed with timber and the vault of the aisle near the king's tomb and chantry were complete. His tomb of black touchstone was only partially built – he surely did not think he would be of need of it as soon as he did.[4] Then with great ceremony the following day, Edward IV was laid to rest. His young son, and England's new king, was on his way to London and what should have happened next was a simple transition of the crown.

But what did happen next, and the events of the next few weeks and months are amongst the most debated and intriguing in history and led to Richard Duke of Gloucester becoming one of our most notorious historical figures. Labelled a usurper and a potential child murderer, he was front and centre of one of history's greatest unsolved mysteries – that of the Princes in the Tower.

A debate had been raging in the days after Edward's death as to how many men should escort the new young king from Ludlow. According to the Croyland Chronicle, there was concern amongst many that the new king should not fall under the complete control of the queen's family. He particularly mentions Hastings and that 'The advice of the lord Hastings, the Captain of Calais, at last prevailed, who declared that he himself would fly thither with all speed, rather than await the arrival of the new king, if he did not come attended by a moderate escort. For he was afraid lest, if the supreme power should fall into the hands of the queen's relations, they would exact a most signal vengeance for the injuries which had been formerly inflicted on them by that same lord; in consequence of which, there had long existed extreme ill-will between the said lord Hastings and the Quene'.[5]

The writer of the chronicle tells how the queen heeded the worry of the councillors and wrote to her son requesting he made his way to London with an escort not exceeding 2000 men. At around the same time Richard of Gloucester replied from his home in Middleham by sending 'loving letters to Elyzabeth the Quene, comforting hir with many woords and promising his allegiance and to increase the credit of his carefulness and natural affection towards his brother's children'.[6] He also commanded all his men to swear obedience to Prince Edward. It seems at this point that all was going well and according to plan.

Gloucester set out on the long journey down from his home in the north of England to London. Simultaneously Edward's young son had set off from Ludlow and was being escorted to the capital by his older brother Richard Grey, and his uncle, Anthony Woodville, Earl Rivers, both who had been with the young prince at Ludlow. The Duke of Buckingham, who was married to Katherine Woodville, the queen's sister, met up with Gloucester along his route and on 29th April they spent the evening in Northampton, sharing a convivial meal with Rivers and Richard Grey who had ridden to meet them there. The new young king did not join them for the meal but remained behind at Stony Stratford. By all accounts all four men enjoyed each other's company that evening. However, the next day, 30th April, they all began their journey to meet up with the new king at Stony Stratford, eighteen miles south of Northampton. But before they reached the town, Gloucester and Buckingham pulled their horses up and informed Rivers and Richard Grey that they were under arrest. The two Dukes then rode off to meet Edward to escort him to London themselves, ordering Rivers and Grey to be taken to one of Gloucester's northern castles as prisoners.[7]

What instigated this action is unclear, but hearing this news, the queen back in London realised something was terribly wrong and for the second time in her life, Elizabeth once again fled into the sanctuary of Westminster Abbey, with her daughters and her younger son Prince Richard. Dorset also initially took sanctuary alongside his mother. Cecily's whereabouts at this time are unknown. Wherever she was, this news following shortly after messages delivering news of the death of the king, must have left her shocked and confused.

The new King Edward soon arrived in London, escorted by his uncle, Gloucester and the Duke of Buckingham, where preparations for the young king's coronation had already begun. However, on their arrival, the coronation was immediately delayed. Events then moved surprisingly quickly. The council pronounced Richard Lord Protector, not a particularly surprising move due to the new king's young age. On 10th and 11th June Gloucester wrote to the City of York and to Lord Neville (his mother's family) asking them to bring troops 'to aid and assist us against the queen, her bloody adherents and affinity, which have intended and daily doth intend to murder and utterly destroy us and our cousin the Duke of Buckingham and the old royal blood of the realm.'[8]

Edward was given rooms in the Tower of London where he would stay whilst awaiting his coronation. It was agreed by the council that Edward's younger brother Richard should also be bought to join him there. Knowing that the queen may not release her other son willingly, Gloucester surrounded their sanctuary with troops. Afraid that if she did not surrender her younger son, Richard would take him by force, the queen reluctantly agreed to let him go and join his elder brother, trusting the word of the Archbishop of Canterbury that he would be returned to her after the coronation. Not long after Richard joined his brother, the boys were moved into apartments further within the tower. Mancini tells of how they were seen less frequently through bars and windows, and that all their servants were soon dismissed until eventually they were no longer seen at all. Mancini also alleges that Gloucester stopped wearing mourning and started wearing purple, the colour of royalty. One of the last attendants to see the boys was their physician John Argentine, who according to Mancini reported that Prince Edward daily sought remission of his sins because he believed that death was facing him. Mancini was reporting this second or third hand so we cannot be sure that the statement that Edward was aware of his impending death is fact or embellishment. Whether the new king considered himself captive or just believed he was awaiting his coronation is unknown and may have changed as time went on. It is likely that in the first instance, he trusted his uncle and did believe he would be king. How quickly that changed, would depend on what their fate actually was and how soon he became aware of it and is part of the integral mystery of their disappearance.

June 22nd, which was the newly arranged coronation day of Edward V came and went. Publicly accusations had been made that Edward IV's marriage to Elizabeth was invalid as he was already pre-contracted to an Eleanor Butler, followed by even more salacious rumours that Edward IV was a bastard son, a result of his mother's affair, a hugely controversial claim considering Cecily Neville, mother to both Edward and Richard, was still alive. Eventually a coronation did take place on 6th July, but it was not that of Edward V, instead Londoners witnessed the coronation of Richard of Gloucester and his wife, Anne Neville. The late Earl of Warwick's wish had finally come true; he had a daughter on the throne of England. And England had a surprising new king – Richard III.

This unexpected turn of events had personal repercussions for Cecily. Not only were her young nephews missing, presumed dead, her mother-in-law confined in sanctuary, grieving, and worried for the future of herself and her daughters but her husband, now a wanted man, was also in hiding. As if this were not enough, just a few weeks before Gloucester claimed the throne, Cecily would have received news of the murder of her stepfather, Hastings.

William Hastings, eternally loyal to Edward IV, had unsurprisingly kept his word and transferred his loyalty to his young son. This unswerving loyalty may have been what ultimately led to his death, in perhaps one of the most shocking and least understood acts that Gloucester was to commit during these few months. The events leading up to Hastings' death took place on 13th June. Gloucester called a council meeting on that day and according to Vergil, he invited some of the nobles to a meeting at the tower, and others to a meeting at Westminster, supposedly to discuss Edward's coronation. A seemingly unsuspecting Hastings attended the tower and the meeting began congenially. A short while into the proceedings, Gloucester allegedly requested that the Bishop of Ely who was also present, return to his garden at Holborn to pick them some of his excellent strawberries. The Bishop agreed to send for some, and Gloucester excused himself and left the room.[9]

Returning shortly after, his earlier amiable mood had now turned sour. Demanding of the gathered men what punishment they thought should be meted out to any who threatened his life, it is reported that Hastings replied that anyone who threatened the life of the Protector should be treated as a traitor and punished accordingly. Gloucester then declared that the traitors he spoke of were 'the sorceress, my brother's wife (referring to Queen Elizabeth Woodville), and Jane Shore, his mistress, with others, their associates'. Citing witchcraft, he apparently revealed his arm to the group of men, which he claimed had been withered away by sorcery. He then accused Hastings of colluding with the women and slamming his hand down upon the table, he gave a cry of treason, causing a retinue of armed men to storm into the room. Hastings was dragged from the room and out onto a patch of grass within the tower, where without judgement or trial he was beheaded.[10] Three other men were also seized with him that day: Lord Stanley and the Bishops of York and Ely. The two Bishops were initially thrown into prison and Stanley was only released when his son arrived to rescue him. Later Bishop Morton, Bishop of Ely was taken to Raglan as a prisoner of the

Duke of Buckingham, and the Bishop of York was put into the care of Sir James Tyrell. The very same day that this took place, Gloucester sent orders to Pontefract that the queen's other son, Richard Grey, and her brother Anthony, should be executed.

The reason for Hastings' murder has never been established. The best explanation is that Gloucester knew that his loyalty to Edward IV would never have allowed him to support his claim to the throne. Perhaps he did also believe (or know) that Hastings was sheltering Jane Shore and believed either one or both of them were conspiring with the queen. Gloucester and Hastings had both given tireless loyalty to Edward IV during his reign and as a result must have spent much time together. With a common cause you would expect them to be allies and even friends, but maybe a deeper rivalry had existed between them for a while, perhaps competing over the years for Edward's attention.

After Edward's death, Jane Shore, must have been bereft. In her role as king's mistress, she would have wanted for nothing. With Edward's sudden death she would have found herself alone and lonely, and in need of a protector. It is alleged that after Edward's death Hastings took up residence in her house. From this distance of time, we can never know the facts of their relationship, but perhaps he was the honourable man that More had described him as and he purely wished to protect her. If she were Dorset's mistress at this time, she could have been involved in transferring messages backwards and forwards to both the queen and Dorset in sanctuary. Gloucester may not have been too far from the truth about her collusion with the queen – two women who should have been natural enemies, coming together in a common cause, bound together by their love for the same men, both the late king and Dorset. The horrific news of Hastings' murder when it reached Cecily must have been heart-breaking and Cecily would have grieved for herself and been hugely worried for her mother. Richard III has his supporters and detractors, but whatever your stance, his behaviour surrounding the death of Hastings is hard to justify.

William Hastings had written a Will on 27th June 1481. In it, he had named Katherine, his wife of over twenty years, as executor, alongside his eldest son Edward, who was around seventeen years old at the time of his father's death, and two other gentlemen – Sir William Husee and Richard Pigotte. He began, as was the norm, by bequeathing his soul into the care of Almighty God, before stating his burial wishes. The closeness of his friendship with Edward IV is never better illustrated than by the fact that Edward had offered Hastings a burial place alongside him in the chapel of St George at Windsor. In his Will Hastings requests to be buried there 'as his Grace had willed and offred'.[11] Despite the circumstances of his death, Richard III, perhaps with a semblance of remorse, honoured his wishes and Hastings was buried near to the master he had faithfully served for twenty-two years.

As also detailed in his Will, Hastings left the care of his children to Katherine, who were all still teenagers or younger at the time of his death. He remembered his immediate family, bequeathing money to his sister and his nieces for their marriages and left provision for his daughter Anne's marriage to his ward, George Earl of Shrewsbury as well as leaving her plate to the value of fifty marks and bedding. His elder sons were left various manors, although the eldest, Edward Hastings, would inherit the bulk of them after his mother died. To all his younger sons he also left plate and bedding 'and other stuff convenient for them'.[12]

To Katherine he left several manors including Stoke Daubeny, Welberston and Sutton in Northamptonshire, the manor of Edmonton in Tottenham and of course their homeland estates of Kirby, Ashby, Bagworth and Thornton and their surrounding parkland. In his Will, written during the reign of Edward IV, he makes a poignant request to his king and good friend, in the event that he died before his king that 'in most humble wise, beseche the king's grace to take the governannce of my son and heir and, as straitly as to me is possible, I charge myne heir on my blessing, to be faythfull and true to the king's grace, to my Lord Prince and their heires, &c'.[13] His loyalty to his king was steadfast and sadly in the end probably proved his undoing. Cecily is not mentioned in his Will, but this is no slight on their relationship; she was already by then a married woman, with her own income and therefore well provided for.

William Hastings was laid to rest in what is now known as The Hastings chapel within St George's chapel. His body lies in a cage chantry which stands in the fourth bay of the north choir aisle of St George's, two bays to the west of the tomb of Edward IV.[14] The origins of St George's chapel date back to around 1350 and was begun by Edward III for his Garter Knights. The construction of the new chapel at St George's was started by Edward IV immediately after he recovered the throne in 1471. The king had selected Windsor as his last resting place rather than the family mausoleum at Fotheringhay in Northamptonshire or Westminster Abbey where previous kings were buried. St George's was intended to be a grand and ornate space for use by Edward both during his lifetime and after his death and from the very beginning it was intended to include several distinct chantry chapels.

As the founder and patron of the chapel, the souls of Edward IV and his queen would benefit from all the masses that were celebrated there, but in addition he still founded a separate chantry within this building devoted personally to the benefit of his soul, with two chantry priests. Unfinished as it was when Edward and Hastings were laid to rest there, it was finally completed by the Tudor monarchs during the late fifteenth and early-sixteenth centuries.

Although Gloucester honoured Hastings' wish to be buried in the chapel, it was only under the authority of Henry VII that Katherine and their eldest son Edward finally managed to achieve the full execution of his Will in respect of the chantry foundation. Hastings' Will provided for a chantry priest who would sing masses and pray for his soul and these were not in place until 1498, when chantry priests were receiving their full £8 salary per year. A monument was also reportedly erected by Katherine and Edward, although no surviving evidence of it exists. The foundation deed was signed by his son and is dated 30th November 1499. The deed is now held in the chapel archives.[15]

After her husband's death, in what must have been a hard letter to write, but knowing she needed to safeguard herself and her family, an emotionally battered and bruised Katherine wrote to the new king. Perhaps bearing some guilt, he replied, promising to be a good Lord to the family and allowing Katherine to retain the wardship of her son, Cecily's stepbrother Edward, who was now the new Lord Hastings. The new King had initially confiscated Hastings' estates but in July he removed the attainder and restored the estates to Katherine, except for Loughborough, which he said belonged to Queen Anne Neville.[16] One of Richard's associates, Francis Lord Lovell, also made a claim to the manors of Ashby and Bagworth but after much contention a monetary agreement was reached. Several years later, when Henry VII took the throne, he restored full possession of all the Hastings estates to Edward Hastings.

Having successfully dispatched Hastings and taken the throne, Richard III was now intent on finding Dorset and rounding up all the remaining Woodvilles. Hearing reports of what had happened to his father-in-law, Dorset realised that sanctuary may not be enough to protect him and at some point he escaped from the abbey confines. Completely unaware of his whereabouts, the king targeted Jane Shore; he at least was under the impression that she and Dorset were or had been lovers. Suspecting Jane had been harbouring him, but unable to locate

Dorset with her, she received the full extent of his anger. Jane was arrested and made to do public penance. Deemed a harlot, she was forced to walk barefoot through the streets dressed only in her kirtle and carrying a candle before being thrown into prison. Allegedly, although this punishment was designed to humiliate her, as she paraded through the streets, the people of London took pity on her and were won over by her beauty and humility.

During the next few months, Dorset remained undetected, very possibly hiding out at one of his properties in the south. On 23rd October King Richard issued a proclamation offering a reward of 1000 marks in money or 100 marks a year in land for taking Thomas 'late marquis of Dorset' who 'not having the fear of God, nor the salvation of his own soul, before his eyes, had damnably debauched and defiled many maids, widows, and wives, and lived in actual adultery with the wife of Shore'.[17] The news of her missing husband (if indeed she had no idea where he was) must have been upsetting to Cecily, and even more so if news of the king's proclamation had reached her ears detailing her husband's alleged infidelity.

Cecily and Dorset's relationship is impossible to dissect from this distance of time. Whether they loved each other or despised each other can only ever be guessed at. They did have many children together, which suggests there was an intimacy between them and many couples who were strangers when they were married developed a close bond over time, through shared experiences; some would even be lucky enough to find love. If Dorset was licentious throughout his marriage, particularly during the reign of his stepfather, he managed to be discreet enough as other than his alleged liaison with Jane Shore, he had no other known mistresses. Whether Cecily knew if he had been unfaithful is again a question that has to remain unanswerable. He certainly had plenty of opportunity, spending time at court whilst she remained in Devon raising her children. Like many women of the age, if she did know or suspect, it was likely something she knew she just had to live with as did many other women – her mother-in-law the queen being a prime example. Elizabeth Woodville would have learned to turn a blind eye to her husband's womanising ways and in the next century a later queen, Anne Boleyn, would be reprimanded by King Henry VIII upon complaining of his infidelity that she should 'shut her eyes as her betters had done before her'.

Christine Pisan, in her book *The Treasure of the City of Ladies*, written in 1405, advises women on how to deal with their husband's adultery. Christine was the first professional female writer in Europe and was a respected source on many things, including questions of morality. She advises that every married woman should respect their husband and live in peace with him. She points out that certainly not all men are deserving of their wives' love. Sometimes a man may behave rudely or stray into a love affair. But if the wife cannot remedy the situation, she must put up with this and dissimulate wisely, pretending she does not notice it. Because a prudent woman knows that speaking harshly to him will gain nothing. This advice is not given to take away a woman's pride, in fact quite the opposite. By being pleasant and kind to her husband whilst he is behaving so badly, she will secure herself a moral victory. Christine councils that if the man does not change his ways, the woman should take refuge in God and be resigned to the situation. For at some point, the husband will feel remorse at how he has treated his faithful wife and eventually she will have won her cause through steadfast enduring.[18] Cecily, along with countless other women, may have followed this advice, although if Richard's proclamation reached her ears, it may still have hurt to hear of her husband's alleged infidelity being publicly proclaimed in this way.

As well as offering the reward for Dorset's capture, the king also began to confiscate his property. Thankfully for Cecily, and perhaps also a relief for Dorset himself, Cecily's inheritance could not be touched. At some point, between June and October, Dorset arrived back in Exeter, where perhaps a fraught reunion occurred between husband and wife, although after the fate of Hastings, Cecily would almost certainly have been relieved to see her husband safe and well.

Richard III had been fully supported in his taking of the throne by the Duke of Buckingham. But during the weeks after the coronation something changed dramatically. During September 1483, Richard was on progress in the north. On 24th of that month, for reasons unknown, Buckingham defected, leaving Richard and returning to his home in Brecon. Whilst there, it is thought that he was persuaded by John Morton, Bishop of Ely, to turn coat. John Morton had been an important part of Edward IV's court and was an executor of his Will. He had been held in custody at the Duke's home in Brecon since the infamous council meeting that led to Hastings' death. It is thought that John Morton put the Duke in touch with Queen Elizabeth, who had not been inactive in sanctuary, but who had been plotting with Margaret Beaufort. Margaret Beaufort was a great-granddaughter of John of Gaunt and his mistress and later third wife. Katherine Swynford. As a descendant of Edward III, her son, Henry Tudor, had a tenuous claim to the throne, and had been in exile in France since 1471. By 1483, he was the most senior Lancastrian alive with a claim to the throne. Henry was also the grandson of Catherine of Valois, mother of Henry VI, through her second marriage to Owen Tudor.

Through messages that were smuggled from Margaret into the sanctuary precincts, some by her physician, Lewis Caerleon, and others, perhaps, by Jane Shore, Margaret Beaufort and Elizabeth Woodville had formulated a plan to marry the eldest York princess, Elizabeth, who was in sanctuary with her mother, to Margaret's son, Henry Tudor. Elizabeth Woodville, who we can only assume at this stage either knew both her sons were dead or had no idea of what had become of them, had nothing to lose but to throw in her lot with Margaret and attempt to remove her brother-in-law from the throne.

From his home in Brecon, Buckingham wrote to the exiled Henry Tudor asking him to bring an army to assist in overthrowing Richard. He then began to do the same himself, assembling men and arms at Brecon castle. By Saturday 18th October, he was ready to move, aiming to meet up with Dorset, who had raised the standard of rebellion in Exeter. But nature was to prove a valiant enemy, and in a flood of torrential rain Buckingham reached the River Severn to discover the banks had burst and had to turn back. Many of his men, who had never been that keen to fight in the first place, turned around and returned to their homes.

Having to quickly revise his plans, the Duke decided to make his way to Weobley in Herefordshire, to the home of Lord Ferrers. From Weobley, Buckingham continued to attempt to raise an army, but the men of Herefordshire would not rise, hearing reports that the king and his army were on their way. By this time, Buckingham was a wanted man with a reward on his head. His castle in Wales had been raided and seized by members of the Vaughan family, loyal to the king, who looted the castle and took his daughters into their custody. Realising he was in trouble he disguised his eldest son, who had travelled with him, as a girl and had him smuggled away by loyal retainers. Buckingham and his wife Katherine then went into hiding in Shropshire in the house of a servant, Ralph Bannister. But Bannister sold them out and on 1st November the Duke was captured and taken to the king at Salisbury, where the following day he was beheaded in the marketplace, without trial. Katherine and her younger son were taken to London into custody.

Elizabeth Woodville's brothers, Lionel and Richard Woodville had also aligned themselves with the rebels alongside Thomas

St Leger, Anne of York's second husband, who took up arms against his brother-in-law the king. Unaware of Buckingham's capture and subsequent death, rebels at Bodmin declared Henry Tudor king. Henry Tudor had set sail from France as requested, but as he neared the English coast, he sensed luck was not on his side and his small fleet turned and sailed back to Brittany. Dorset, hearing the news of Buckingham's fate and Henry Tudor's retreat, realised he himself had little choice but to flee the country himself and he crossed the channel to join Henry and his men.

The rebellion had failed. Richard III would remain on the throne of England for the next two years whilst the Tudor camp regrouped on French shores, planning their next move. During this time, it is highly likely that Cecily lived quietly in Devon raising her family. She may also have travelled to spend some time with her mother and comfort her in her grief. Her relationship with her mother-in-law is unknown, but perhaps she also communicated with her during these months, perhaps discreetly sharing news with each other of Dorset in France.

On 1st March 1484, a few months after Dorset had fled the country, Elizabeth Woodville and her daughters left the sanctuary confines after she struck an agreement with Richard III that her girls would come to no harm. Initially the girls were released into the care of the king and queen, probably entering the household of Queen Anne Neville at Westminster, the only place suitable for young unmarried girls at court. When Elizabeth Woodville left the abbey precincts a short time later, she was entrusted into the keeping of Sir John Nesfield, and housed at one of his properties, most likely at Hertford Castle or Heytesbury manor. Her daughters most likely joined her there when not at court. The fate of her sons, the two princes, has never been established nor is it known whether Elizabeth Woodville knew or ever found out what happened to her two boys.

Although the initial struggles had been fought and Richard had seemingly emerged the victor, the plans for Henry Tudor to come to England were merely delayed. But in an unexplained turn of events, in 1485 Elizabeth Woodville wrote to her son, Dorset, urging him to leave Henry Tudor and return home where he would be well received by the king. Richard Woodville, another of the rebels, had been pardoned by Richard III on 30th March of that year. Why this letter was sent is a puzzle. Dorset, seemingly decided to take his mother's advice, and slipped away from Henry Tudor's camp under the cover of darkness. Concerned that he knew too many of their secrets, Henry dispatched a gentleman named Humphrey Cheyne to chase after him and bring him back. Dorset was found quite easily and Melita Thomas, the author of *The House of Grey* suggests that perhaps that was the intention – to give the impression to the king that he was returning but never actually intending to succeed in his desertion. So whichever way the tide turned, Dorset could claim that he was on that side. Dorset returned to camp and remained with the rebels until finally, after many months of planning, Henry Tudor once again set sail for England, landing in Milford Haven on 7th August 1485. Not being able to raise enough money to equip his army, Tudor borrowed heavily from the Captain of the Bastille, Philippe Luillier. In return for the loan, he was obliged to pledge all his personal belongings and as Edward IV did during his French campaign, he was also required to leave behind two men as a pledge that he would keep his word and repay his debts. The two men left behind on French shores were Sir John Bourchier and the Marquis of Dorset. Henry Tudor also had to agree to pay for their upkeep at the Bastille during their time there. Both men, as Knights of the Garter, also provided their own letters of assurances.

Richard III, aware that Henry Tudor was now in England and ready to challenge him for the throne, gathered his army and made his way to meet him. The two armies finally met on Bosworth field on 22nd August 1485. Ever a good soldier, even Richard's detractors agree that he fought bravely, but it was not enough. The king was defeated, and his body was thrown naked upon a horse and taken to buried at the Grey Friars in Leicester, a Franciscan priory, where his remains were discovered nearly three hundred years later in 2012 in the fascinating archaeological dig that found the remains of 'the king in the car park'.

Heading straight to London after his victory, Henry Tudor was crowned king of England on 30th October 1485. Dorset and Bourchier who had been left behind in France returned to England's shores, arriving back sometime before Christmas, although not in time for the king's coronation. England could once again hope for a period of stability. Richard, Duke of Gloucester and then King Richard III, had played a huge part in the lives of many, first as a loyal brother to King Edward, then as a usurper of the throne. His defeat, celebrated as it was by many, must have been bittersweet to others, reflecting on the surprising events of the last few years. But for Cecily and her family, they could now get on and look forward to the rest of their lives. Cecily had her husband back safe and sound and the Tudor era had begun.

Chapter Five

The Early Tudor years

1485-1501

Christmas 1485 saw the Dorset family back together for the Yule celebrations for the first time in three years. England had now had several months to adjust to a new king on the throne and an end to the rule of the great Plantagenet kings. Henry Tudor was not only a new king, but he was also the first of a new dynasty. Declaring the start of his reign from the day before the battle of Bosworth, he ensured that all those who fought on Richard's side would be classed as traitors.

Whatever Dorset's relationship had been with Jane Shore, by the time he was back in the country in late 1485, Jane had been freed from prison and in an unpredicted turn of events, she was now a married woman. Whilst languishing in Ludgate prison, Jane had met a gentleman named Thomas Lynam. Thomas was the king's solicitor who had visited her during her detention, and it seems that even at her least attractive in a prison cell, the charms that had won over a king shone through and the pair fell in love. King Richard, perhaps deciding she had been punished enough, agreed to the union, although not without expressing his disbelief. Writing to Bishop Russell in 1483, Richard mentioned the pending marriage: 'signifying unto you that I showed unto us that our servant and solicitor Thomas Lynam, marvellously blinded and abused with the late [wife] of William Shore, now being in Ludgate by our commandment, hath made contract of matrimony with her, as it is said, and intendeth to our full great marvel, to proceed to effect the same. We for many causes would be sorry that he should be so disposed. Pray you therefore to send for him, and in that you goodly may exhort and stir him to the contrary. And if you find him utterly set for to marry her and none other will be advertised, if it may stand with the laws of the church, we be content, the time of the marriage being deferred to our coming next to London, that on sufficient surety being found of her good bearing, ye do send for her keeper and discharge him of our said commandment, by warrant of these committing her to the rule and guiding of her father or any other by your direction in the mean season.[1] Presumably, whatever relationship had occurred between Dorset and Jane was now well and truly over. Jane and Thomas Lynam would go on to have a child together, and Jane herself survived well into her seventies outliving most of her contemporaries. Thomas More writing in his *History of King Richard III* in 1513, discussed her wit and beauty with the aside 'and yet she liveth'.[2] There is even a suggestion that he may have met her or at least seen her in person. She is believed to have died around 1527/28.

Upon his return to England, Dorset's attainder was reversed by King Henry and his title of Marquis restored. The king also awarded him a grant of £35 per annum and a place on his council. As well as having his own lands returned to him, Dorset had also acquired new lands during his sojourn in France, when his grandmother Elizabeth, Lady Ferrers, had died. As well as inheriting the family lands and estates, Dorset also now held the title Lord Ferrers of Groby.[3] But Dorset would never fully enjoy Henry Tudor's trust. He was stripped of many of the wardships and grants that he had received under Edward IV, including having to surrender the wardship of the Earl of Warwick, which may have been a particular cause of sadness to Cecily. She must have been hugely upset at the loss of the young boy who she likely became close to during his time in her household. The king clearly did not fully trust the man who had seemingly attempted to desert him whilst they were in exile. This mistrust may have been down to his attempt to flee Henry's camp in

France, but it also may just have been a sensible move by the king, still so new to the throne. Henry Tudor was well aware that there were still some male Yorkists alive with a legitimate claim to the throne, including Edward Earl of Warwick and the Earl of Lincoln (John de la Pole) and his brothers, the sons of Elizabeth Plantagenet. It would have been naive for Henry to not be wary of them. Dorset, as the son of Queen Elizabeth Woodville, may just have fallen into the same category. Upon leaving the Dorset household, the Earl of Warwick was placed straight into the tower by Henry. Still only a young lad, Henry no doubt wanted him out of the way of those Yorkist sympathisers who may have been tempted to use him for their own cause.

The plans put into place all those years before by Elizabeth Woodville and Henry's mother, Margaret Beaufort, finally came to fruition in January 1486 with the wedding of Henry and the Princess Elizabeth of York, Dorset's half-sister. The wedding took place on 18th January 1486, finally uniting the houses of York and Lancaster after all the years of conflict. The young Princess Elizabeth was nineteen, her husband to be a full ten years older at the age of twenty-nine. Elizabeth wore a wedding dress of silk damask and crimson satin with a kirtle of white cloth of gold damask and a mantle furred with ermine to protect her from the winter weather. Her loose blonde hair was threaded with jewels. The marriage ceremony took place in Westminster Abbey, and the people of England rejoiced, hoping this was actually the new beginning they had hoped for and an end to the troubles of the past thirty years. Fires were lit far and wide and the people of London and no doubt those across the country revelled with dances, songs and feasts. But despite the agreement to make her queen, her coronation would not take place for nearly another two years.

She may not yet have been crowned but Elizabeth did fulfil her wifely duties, and just over eight months after their wedding nuptials, in September 1486, she gave birth to their first son and the new Tudor heir – a prince they named Arthur. The young prince was christened on the Sunday after his birth, the event reportedly being delayed because one of the godfathers, the Earl of Oxford, needed to return from Suffolk for the occasion, a journey which may have been slowed down due to the wet weather the country was experiencing at the time.[4] Both Cecily and Dorset were invited, and Dorset seemed to have, for a while, been forgiven for his escape attempt, as both were given honoured roles in the service.

Arthur's christening took place in the cathedral church of Winchester. Both the young Prince's chosen Christian name and the choice of location for his birth and christening, were designed to illustrate the power of the new Tudor regime. Winchester was the home of the legendary King Arthur, and by association it invoked a sense of awe and majesty that this new dynasty of Tudor kings would bring to the country. The church was decked out in all its finery, with the main body of the church awash with rich arras cloth that had been hung for the occasion. The day began with a procession headed up by yeomen carrying unlit torches. Behind them came the men and women of the court. The queen's sister, Lady Cecily of York, was given the honour of carrying baby Arthur.[5] The baby prince, completely oblivious to the importance of the occasion, was wrapped in a mantle of crimson cloth of gold, furred with ermine, with a train, which was supported by Cecily Dorset. Dorset accompanied the ladies along with the Earl of Lincoln, who it seemed at this point was also welcome at the Tudor court.

The christening party proceeded through the cloisters of the Abbey through a little door into the southern part of the church. Leland tells us that the weather was too cold and foul for the ceremony to take part in the west end. Waiting at the font to welcome her grandson was Elizabeth Woodville. According to Leland, the gathered guests were informed at this point that the Earl of Oxford was a mere mile away, hastening to the church as fast as he could. Several hours later, upon the orders of the king and probably much to the relief of all present, the Bishop of Worcester performed the christening without the Earl's presence as he had still not arrived. The Earl of Derby and Lord Maltravers, the husband of one of Elizabeth Woodville's sisters, were godfathers at the font, and Queen Elizabeth Woodville stood as godmother. Shortly after the Prince was christened, and the Officers of Arms had put on their coats and lit the torches, the Earl of Oxford finally made his appearance, just in time to witness the young Prince being confirmed by the Bishop of Exeter.

The prince was then returned in procession to his parents, once again carried by his aunt, the Lady Cecily. As they entered the royal nursery, they were met by the king's trumpeters and minstrels playing their instruments. Arthur was then returned to his parents for their blessing and as was the custom, his mother was the first one to call him by his name. For the honoured guests, the celebrations continued for the rest of the day with Leland reporting that in the churchyard there were 'Pipes of Wyne, that every Man myght drynke ynows'.[6]

Whatever words were shared between Cecily and her husband upon his return about past events, the couple were clearly reunited in all ways by now as Cecily had also fallen pregnant again, with another son George being born the same year as Prince Arthur, followed by two further daughters – Cecily in c.1487 and Dorothy in c.1488.

The first year of Henry's reign had begun peacefully enough and without challenge. But trouble was never going to be far away, with pockets of Yorkist supporters still in existence, and the first disruption to Henry's kingship once again had a direct effect on the Dorsets. In the spring of 1487, a young man came to the palace's attention, proclaiming his right to the English throne. Managing to convince others of his claim, he had himself crowned Edward, King of England, on 27th May 1487 in Christ

Church, Dublin. His supporters claimed that the man they had crowned king was Edward Earl of Warwick, Clarence's son, whom they argued had a stronger right to the throne than Henry Tudor. Even though he had been barred from the accession due to the attainder and execution of his father, the young Earl probably did have a strong claim. But in 1487, Warwick was just eleven or twelve years old. Rumoured to be a weak lad, perhaps even with some form of mental disability, he was no candidate for a strong king of England. He was also nowhere near Dublin, but still locked up in the Tower of London.

Henry soon learned of the involvement of the Earl of Lincoln in this plot as well as Margaret of Burgundy, Lincoln's aunt, who had agreed to send troops in support. Lincoln and Francis Lovell, Richard III's old associate, had arrived in Dublin just before the coronation accompanied by 2000 of Margaret's troops. They then set sail for England with their 'new king', arriving ten days later in Lancashire where they made land and began their march south. As a precaution against the arrival of further of Margaret's men, Henry made the decision to fortify the whole east coast. He set off to Bury St Edmunds, leaving the queen and Prince Arthur in the safety of Kenilworth Castle, to personally see this was done.

In a bizarre set of circumstances, it seems Dorset was also headed towards the East coast at the same time. His reasons for travelling there are unclear but when questioned he told them he was visiting the Shrine of St Edmund.

Residing in the Abbey Church of Bury St Edmunds, the shrine was a place of pilgrimage during the middle ages and it was here that Dorset alleged he was heading. St Edmund had been the king of East Anglia from AD 855 to 869. Beheaded by Danish invaders for refusing to denounce Christianity, his body had later been found without its head. Hunting for the king's head, his men had been attracted by a wolf call. They followed the sound and came across a wolf guarding the decapitated head. Upon re-uniting the head and body they miraculously fused back together.

Henry, ever suspicious of Dorset's loyalty, had him apprehended by the Earl of Oxford and taken to the tower. According to Francis Bacon, 'He sent the Earl of Oxford to meet [Dorset] to accompany him back to London and forthwith to carry him to the Tower; with a fair message nevertheless that he should bear that disgrace with patience, for that the king meant not his hurt, but only to preserve him from doing hurt either to the king's service or to himself'.[7] What Dorset's real motives were for this trip to the East Coast we will never know. Was it just an inconvenient coincidence that the rebels disturbed his pilgrimage or was he actually involved in the plot to remove Henry? It would seem unlikely that he was unaware that his old ward was actually being held in London, or that he would make a move against his half-sister, for to remove Henry from the throne would also remove Elizabeth and Arthur.

To prevent the rebellion from spreading, Henry also had the real Earl of Warwick bought from the tower and paraded through the streets of London. Lincoln, Lovell and their army finally met up with the king's men on 16th June on the battlefield at Stoke. Henry emerged victorious. The Earl of Lincoln was killed in the fighting and Lord Lovell fled when it became clear they were defeated. Where he fled to is a mystery, although legend tells that he eventually ended up in his house at Minster Lovell, where he was hidden by a servant in a secret underground chamber. It is said that in the early 18th century, during building work at the Hall, an underground room was discovered. In this room a skeleton was found, sitting upright at a table, surrounded by books, paper and pens. According to the tale, the loyal servant died before Lovell, and with no one else knowing he was there, Lovell was unable to escape the room from the inside and starved to death.

Whatever Dorset's motives were for his East Coast trip, other close members of his family did turn out to fight for the king including Cecily's half-brother, Edward Lord Hastings and Edward Woodville, Dorset's uncle. The imposter 'Warwick' was captured and revealed to be a young man called Lambert Simnel. It is said that Henry took pity on the young lad and he was taken to London and given a job in the royal kitchens.

At around the same time as the Simnel affair was taking place, Queen Elizabeth Woodville retired to the Abbey of Bermondsey. This led to rumours that she too was involved in the plotting and that the king had forced her to retire to the Abbey where she would be unable to cause trouble. Again, her involvement along with Dorset's is all conjecture and it seems unlikely that they would risk Elizabeth's position for a young lad not even of their blood. What was actually going on and how much Cecily was aware of the activities of her husband and mother-in-law can only be speculated on. Dorset seems to have remained in the tower for several months after the Simnel affair; he was still there in November 1487 and consequently missed the eventual coronation of his half-sister which eventually took place that month. Cecily is also not listed in the list of ladies in attendance so perhaps with her husband confined, it was not considered appropriate for her to attend either. Although she may have just chosen to remain at home with her family, perhaps she was in some stage of pregnancy or unwell or perhaps she just chose not to attend without her husband.

The new queen, Elizabeth of York, was welcomed by the people, who were joyous to see a daughter of the popular Edward IV become queen. Her coronation festivities took place over several days and began on 24th November when Elizabeth made her state entry into London in a grand procession through the streets of the city. The queen's train was carried by her sister Cecily of York, who rode in a carriage behind the queen alongside Katherine Woodville, the new Duchess of Bedford. Katherine Woodville was the youngest of the Woodville girls and during the reign of Edward IV, had been married to the Duke of Buckingham. She had recently taken Jasper Tudor as her second husband, acquiring the title of duchess. The wedding party spent the night at Westminster, and the following morning, the 25th November, Elizabeth, dressed in purple velvet proceeded to Westminster Abbey accompanied by her ladies. The procession was hugely eventful it seems, with reports that amidst such huge crowds that had formed to try and cut a piece of the woollen floor covering that the queen walked on (as was the custom), a number of people were killed: 'ther was so Hoge a people inordyantly presing to cut the Ray Cloth ... in the presence certeyne Persons were slayne, and the Order of the ladies folowing the Quene was broken and distrobled'.[8] The ceremony was followed by the obligatory banquet, attended by all the great and good of the land. But perhaps much to his dismay, Dorset was not here to witness his sister's joy and triumph.

Dorset was released not long after Elizabeth's coronation, but still found himself under a cloud of mistrust, He was required to give guarantees of loyalty to the crown and to make his eldest son, the ten-year-old Thomas Grey, a ward of the king, giving the king control of whom he would marry. This recent incident along with the incident in France sealed Henry's opinion of him and a few years later, on 4th June 1492, he was obliged to convey his lands to feoffees and to sign an indenture stating that if he committed treason or misprision of treason (concealment of treason), the feoffees would hold the lands for the use of the king.[9]

Excluded more now from the inner circles of the court than they were during Edward IV's reign, the couple may have set their focus on their family life. Over the next few years Dorset and Cecily's family continued to grow and they would go on to parent five further children: Leonard, Mary, Elizabeth, Margaret and their last, Edward, born around 1495. Having made Shute their principal family home, it was during the 1490s that the couple also began renovations of Groby Hall in Leicestershire, the property that Dorset had inherited from his maternal grandmother, although it is not believed that the couple ever lived here, preferring instead to reside at Astley Castle, another Grey family home, when they were in the area.

Groby Hall was situated within a beautiful large park, complete with a lake and to enable him to make the renovations, Dorset at this time made various land exchanges including that of the Woodville family manor at Grafton which he had inherited from his uncle, Earl Rivers. During this same time period, they also began work on a far more impressive house at Bradgate. Bradgate was part of the manor of Groby, within the waste of Charnwood Forest and also came to the Dorsets as part of the Ferrers inheritance. The surrounding parkland around Bradgate had been enclosed since at least the mid thirteenth century and the park was well stocked with deer. Dorset's grand plans were to construct a large brick mansion within the grounds.[10] Sadly, he did not live long enough to see his project reach fruition and the house would eventually be completed by his son, Thomas, who upon Dorset's death would become the second Marquis. Bradgate itself would eventually become synonymous with Cecily and Dorset's great-granddaughter, Lady Jane Grey, who would be born there in 1537 and brought up there. The house had been left to ruin by the middle of the seventeenth century.

The brick mansion that Dorset planned at Bradgate was to be situated in the south-eastern corner of the park. Built in the shape of a 'U', the private apartments were contained in the south wing. The house also featured a chapel and a solar situated off the grand hall. In the grounds of the house there was a tiltyard, a practice ground where Dorset could partake in his love of jousting and perhaps instruct his sons in the sport that he loved so much. To the north of the tiltyard was a triangular fishpond, which powered a mill and provided a water source for the house.

During the 1490s, the couple may well have been splitting their time between Shute Manor and Astley Castle whilst supervising the works at Groby and Bradgate. They also had a mansion house and several other properties in Vintry parish in London, on the north bank of the Thames and near to Southwark Bridge. This substantial mansion house was near Baynards Castle and would have been their base when in London.[11]

From somewhere around the mid-1480s Dorset and Cecily were also involved in a litigation case through the Courts of Chancery that continued into the following decade. The defendants were a gentleman named John Bonville, his wife Katherine and certain others including William Hody, Chief Baron of the Exchequer, in regard to the manors of Shute, Wiscombe and North Leigh in Devon, and certain other of their lands. Details of their disagreement are unclear – the National Archives holds a paper relating to the proceedings, but it is much worn and illegible.[12] Cecily and Dorset were the plaintiffs and the John Bonville in question is likely to have been the son of old William Bonville's brother. Born in 1413, he was a whole generation older than Cecily. He had married Katherine, the daughter of Sir Robert Wingfield. John Bonville died in 1495 so if not resolved beforehand, this may have bought the dispute to a close.[13]

1492 was a particularly sad year for the Dorset family when they received the upsetting news of the death of the Dowager Queen, Elizabeth Woodville. She was around fifty-five years old. Dorset, who had remained close to his mother throughout her life, must have been heartbroken. Elizabeth took her last breaths on Friday 8th June 1492 at Bermondsey, where she had been living in peace and seclusion for the last few years of her life. Her funeral was to be a humble affair for a woman who had been queen but was as she had requested. In her Will she desired to buried at Windsor with her husband, Edward, 'without pompes entring or costlie expensis donne thereabought'. Her journey down river from Bermondsey to Windsor took place on Sunday 10th June. The late queen's body was accompanied by just five attendants, two clerics, Edward Haute, her second cousin, and Grace, an illegitimate daughter of the king's, and an unmarried gentlewoman. Her body was taken through the Little Park at Windsor to St George's chapel. She arrived at 11pm and was met by a single priest and clerk and buried in the tomb immediately. Presumably, the news took time to filter to those close to her, but by the Tuesday mourners were arriving and during the next few days memorial services were held. Cecily arrived with the women on the Tuesday in the company of Bridget, Katherine and Anne of York, as well as several other female relatives. It seems one of her own daughters also accompanied her, most likely the eldest, Eleanor, who would have been around ten years old. The present Queen Elizabeth, her eldest daughter, was indisposed and unable to attend.

On the Tewsday theder came by water iii of kynges Edwardes doughters and heirs, that is to say the lady Anne, the lady Katherine, the lady Bregett, accompeygned by the lady marquys of Dorsset, the Duc of Buckyngham daughter of nyce of the fore said Queen, also the daughter of the marquys of Dorsett...[14]

Dorset himself arrived on the Wednesday and further services were held. Then on Thursday 14th June one of the canons sang the mass of our lady and Dorset offered a gold piece, and a second gold piece at the following mass of the trinity. The ladies did not attend these masses.

Elizabeth Woodville has always been a contentious figure and she and her family still have a bad reputation to contend with even today. She climbed high with her marriage which elevated her to a position where she could be knocked down.

But there is no doubt that her children loved her and they all would have felt her loss keenly. It has never been established whether Elizabeth Woodville eventually discovered the fate of her sons, with many differing theories being touted, including that she had in fact managed to smuggle one or both of them away to safety. But she may simply have died not having any idea of what had become of them. Even those with no love for her would have to acknowledge the personal pain that would have caused her.

A year after his mother's death, Dorset once again found himself journeying to Ludlow Castle where he had been many moons before with his half-brother, Edward. As heir to the throne, it was time for Prince Arthur to be established in his own household, and in 1493 Dorset accompanied him there, an occasion that must also have bought back memories for him of the missing York princes. The king and queen had also enlarged their family since the birth of Prince Arthur, with a daughter Margaret being born in November 1489 and a further son, Henry, in June 1491. Now with an heir and a spare, the royal family had two princes who would be able to continue the line of Tudor kings. As the younger brother, Prince Henry was invested as Duke of York on 27th October 1494 in a ceremony that both Cecily and Dorset attended. Their eldest son, Thomas, was also honoured during the celebrations by being created a Knight of the Bath. A great joust was organised to mark the occasion and as with most royal celebrations the festivities continued for several days. The ceremonies began on the evening of 27th October when the knights waited on the king at supper, before Prince Henry was bathed and dressed in the king's closet. Thomas Grey and another young knight were bathed and dressed in the queen's closet before the remaining knights received the same treatment in the Parliament chamber. Further ceremonies took place the next day, involving the newly created knights and on the third day, the young prince was formerly named Prince of York.[15] After the formalities, the gathered guests proceeded to chapel where they attended mass. This was then followed by a grand procession. The Earl of Shrewsbury carried the new little Duke of York and the king followed further down the line, accompanied by the Dukes of Bedford and Buckingham and Dorset. Cecily was further back, in the train of ladies that were led by the queen. The following days were all spent in celebration, with various jousts and feast which both Dorset and Cecily attended, although an aging Dorset, now approaching forty, did not take part in the jousts as he would have done in his earlier years.

The time had now come for Cecily and Dorset to think about the future of their own children and to start planning their marriages. For one of his daughters, Mary, the second eldest, Dorset purchased the wardship and marriage of Walter Devereux, the son and heir of Lord Ferrers for £200.[16] An agreement was also reached on 20th May 1496 for another of their daughters, their eldest, the Lady Eleanor, to marry Sir John Arundell of Lanherne, a leading man and landowner in Cornwall. She was to have a dowry of 1000 marks and in return an estate of her own, to the value of £20 p.a.

Other than the Simnel affair Henry's kingship had not been seriously threatened. But the most serious threat to his reign was to take place in 1497, although trouble had been rumbling in the background for several years. It began in August 1491, when a young man of refinement sailed into the Irish town of Cork, declaring himself to be Richard of York, the younger of the missing princes in the tower. Worryingly for King Henry, many people believed the story of this sixteen-year-old youth. Unlike Warwick, the fate of Richard of York was unknown. The two princes were believed dead, but without evidence the reappearance of one or both of them could not be discounted. This time there were also many more men unsure what to believe, including some close to the king himself. The strength of the danger to Henry Tudor at this time cannot be underestimated, particularly as even some close to him were ready to believe the story. In an uncomfortable turn of events for his mother, Margaret Beaufort, her husband's brother, Sir William Stanley, was found guilty of supporting the pretender in that he had allegedly been heard to say he would not fight against him if he was the son of Edward IV. Henry had no choice but to arrest Sir William and execute him as an example to all that Henry was not a king to accept disloyalty.

Since his appearance in late 1491, 'Richard' had set sail from Ireland and made his way to France where he managed to gain the support of the French king. He then made his way to Margaret of York's court in Burgundy, where it was reported that she was initially suspicious of her visitor, but later became utterly convinced of his identity and welcomed him with great joy. Over the next few years, the existence of this pretender had caused a shadow over the English court even though Henry had sent his spymasters far and wide to discover his real identity. The officials managed to identify him as a young man called Perkin Warbeck, the son of a peasant couple from Tournai (in modern day Belgium). But even with his supposed identity revealed, he was still a magnet for any disaffected Yorkists.

Through the early 1490s, the existence of this young man had been problematic but had remained a distant threat. However, in July 1495 the pretender had landed in Deal. The men of Kent remained loyal to their king and chased him away. He had subsequently made his way to Scotland where he was received with honours by King James IV, who not only allowed him to live at the Scottish court and treated him as he would a son of Edward IV, but also arranged a suitable marriage for him with a respectable Lady named Katherine Gordon, the daughter of the Earl of Huntly. He was still at the Scottish court on 18th March 1496 when Queen Elizabeth gave birth to her third daughter, Mary, at Sheen. After a further failed attempt to enter

England from the north that same year, he eventually set sail from Scotland in late 1497, making his way to the south coast. Here he found that the men of Cornwall were not as loyal to their king as their Kentish counterparts had been. Disillusioned with Henry VII and his exorbitant taxes, they allowed him to land and march northwards through their lands. Collecting supporters along the way, he had himself declared Richard IV at Bodmin.

The distant threat had now become very real and the king had no choice but to set off to meet his challenger with an army. As the king drew near, many Cornishmen began to desert – a charge of treason was too serious a penalty for them to risk for a man whom they were not even certain was who he said he was. With his supporters fading away and knowing his cause was lost, the pretender went into hiding in Beaulieu Abbey, where he was finally captured. He was taken to Taunton and it was here on 3rd October 1497 that the Tudor king and the alleged York king came face to face for the very first time. Official records tell us he admitted his deception at this meeting when he was put face to face with men he should know. One of these men who came to face him was Dorset, his half-brother. Official records tell us he failed to recognise Dorset and that none of the men present were able to recognise him. Or perhaps would not admit that they recognised him, for some might argue that no good could have come of it if they had admitted to knowing him and he them.

He and his wife Katherine were taken back to London. Lady Katherine Gordon was made one of Elizabeth's ladies and the pretender was allegedly kept close to Henry, not exactly a prisoner but also not at liberty. He later attempted an escape and was captured and thrown into the tower alongside Dorset's old ward, the Earl of Warwick. In a further escape pact between the two men, that was highly likely to have been at least a partial set-up, both Warbeck and Warwick were caught and executed in

November 1498. In one fell swoop, the threat from any male Yorkists was over.

During his time in the south of England in October 1497, King Henry paid a visit to the Dorsets. He had arrived at Taunton on 4th October and having met and dispatched Warbeck back to London, the king then proceeded to Exeter, where he oversaw the hanging of some of the Cornish rebels. He also graciously received the wife of the pretender, Lady Katherine Gordon whilst at Exeter, before she too was sent to London. Leaving Exeter on 3rd November, the king passed the night at Ottery St Mary and then proceeded to Newenham Abbey at Axminster, where he remained for nearly a week until the 10th November. Cecily was patron of both these churches. He is believed to have visited the Dorsets at their home in Shute during this time, where he spent some time in the surrounding deer parks and at leisure, shooting the butts with the Marquis, in the beautiful grounds surrounding their manor house.[17] Perhaps this was an occasion for the king to even the scores as he had previously lost in a game to the Marquis on an earlier occasion in 1495, as detailed in an item in his accounts dated March 20th 1495 – 'Lost at the buttes to my lord marquis, £0 20s 0d'.[18]

The 1490s was also a time when the eldest Grey boys reached school age and several of them were sent to be educated at Magdalen College, in Oxford. According to John Rouse Bloxam, Thomas Grey, along with his brothers, Ambrose, George, and Richard, were noblemen at the College in 1498. Thomas, George and Richard would have been around the ages of twenty-one, twelve and twenty years old, respectively.[19] In the middle ages, students entered university or college once it was deemed that they had the ability to learn, which meant they could be as young as thirteen. So perhaps George Grey was actually thirteen or fourteen in 1498. The Ambrose Grey who is also mentioned is a mystery. It could well have been Anthony Grey who was born c.1483 so would have been fifteen in 1498 and therefore just as likely to have been at Magdalen as his younger brother Richard. Or perhaps he was another Grey son whose details are lost to us.

Magdalen College was a highly respected Oxford school of learning, founded in 1458 by William Waynflete, Bishop of Winchester. With its beautiful cloisters and ivy-mantled quadrangle it was considered to be one of the loveliest houses of learning in England.[20] When approaching the town of Oxford from the east, entrance to the town would have been over a long stately bridge which was adjoined to the tower of the college. As the largest college in Oxford, Magdalen hosted forty fellows and thirty scholars (known at Magdalen as demies).

The original schoolroom built by Bishop Waynflete was seventy-two feet long by twenty-four feet wide and was lit by ten square irregularly placed windows, five on each side, and by two further windows at the east end, of which one was situated over the entrance door. The building of the college had taken several years to complete with the chapel being the first building to be finished. By 1479 the chapel, hall and cloisters were approaching completion, the cloisters lending an area of peace to the surroundings and described as a beautiful, enclosed garden, 'peaceful yet not severe, monastic and domestic at once' which was surrounded by quaint stone figures on pedestals.

The college had received several royal visits since its foundation. When Bishop Waynflete had visited Magdalen in 1481, bringing with him 800 volumes for the library, he set out towards Woodstock two days later where he met King Edward IV. The king made a promise that he would come and visit the newly-built College and spend the night there. Keeping his promise, Edward did visit, reportedly arriving after sunset to be greeted by the Lord Chancellor of the University and the regent and non-regent Master of Arts. He spent the night there and did not leave until after lunch the next day.

Less than two years later the College was once again visited by royalty. Bishop Waynflete, now over eighty years old, came up to Oxford on St Mary Magdalen's Day to receive King Richard III, who toured the college buildings and who stayed two nights this time. On the second day he oversaw debates in the Hall, generously rewarding the winners with gifts of venison and money.[21]

As well as the Grey boys, the college had also educated a young man named Thomas Wolsey, who would later become famous as Cardinal Wolsey, Henry VIII's chief minister. His birth date is unknown, but he is believed to have been born in the early 1470s. He had been awarded one of four scholarships in the gift of the Bishop of Norwich to attend Magdalen, and as an exceptionally intellectual student, he had completed his BA by the age of fifteen. He took a fellowship at the college and was appointed a schoolmaster at Magdalen in 1498, the year the Grey boys were there, a position he only held for six months, before taking on the appointment of College Bursar in 1499.

Dorset was so impressed with Wolsey as a schoolmaster, that in 1500 he invited him to Bradgate for the Christmas festivities. It is even mooted that it may have been through an introduction from his former pupil at Magdalen School, Thomas Grey, that Wolsey would eventually come to the attention of Henry VIII.

But this family Christmas at Bradgate was to be the last as sadly tragedy struck the following year when Thomas, Marquis of Dorset died at the age of just forty-six. He was in London at the time, presumably ailing, as on 30th August 1501 he made his Will. Just three weeks later he was dead. Whether Cecily was with him when he died is unknown but if he was in ill health, she may have had time to reach him and be with him at the end.

In his Will, Dorset stipulated that his body be buried in the collegiate church of Astley in Warwickshire near to their home of Astley Castle. Cecily was named as his executor alongside a neighbouring Leicestershire gentleman, Sir William Skeffington. As any good father would, he left provision for his children, stipulating that each of his unmarried daughters were to receive £1000 towards their dowry. A marriage had recently been agreed between his daughter Cecily and a gentleman named John Dudley – if this failed to proceed, the proportion of the dowry that had already been paid was to be repaid by Lord Sutton, Dudley's father. Groby and Bradgate as well as his lands in Calais were to go to his eldest son Thomas and Astley was left to Cecily as her dower. The title of Marquis also passed to Thomas. Along with the usual bequests, he requested prayers for the soul of his father, for his mother Elizabeth, for Edward IV, for his wife (presumably his first wife, Anne Holland), for his own soul, and for all Christian souls.

Cecily, at the age of forty-two, was now a widow with a large family who still needed her. Her youngest child, Edward, was still only four years old. Financially she was supported, but as with all who lose their spouse, she now had to find a way to move on to the next stage of her life, without the man she had been married to for the last twenty-four years. During their years together, they had been through much and she must have faced the thought of his loss on more than one occasion during the earlier troubled years. But this time it was real, he was gone, and she must continue forward without him.

Chapter Six

Husband Number Two

1501-1530

Upon Dorset's death, his title of Marquis of Dorset, alongside that of the baronies of Groby and Astley were immediately transferred to his eldest son, Thomas Dorset, who was by then a young man of twenty-four. Just over a year later, on 18th November 1502, the new Marquis was granted livery of his lands.[1] Once the funeral was over, a grieving Cecily may have remained at Astley or perhaps even returned to Shute to take some time to mourn her husband and to spend the Christmas period in quiet solitude with her children. She was now facing life as a widow, with the now intricate job of actioning Dorset's Will as well as the prospect that she would now have to raise their large family on her own.

By January 1502 however, most likely still dressed in her black mourning attire, she was back in London to celebrate the proxy wedding of the Scottish King James IV and Princess Margaret at Richmond. Thomas Dorset took part in the celebratory jousts, and perhaps she watched her son with fond memories of times past when she had stood and watched her husband partaking in the sport he enjoyed so much. The ceremony itself took place in the Palace of Richmond, with the Earl of Bothwell standing proxy for James IV. Cecily was in attendance with Queen Elizabeth and the Dowager Duchess of Norfolk. The actual wedding took place the following year when Thomas Dorset accompanied his fourteen-year-old cousin some of the way when she set of for her new life in Scotland.[2]

Cecily's whereabouts for the rest of 1502 are sketchy, although we do find her residing in Lincolnshire towards the end of the year, perhaps to be closer to her mother who by this time was sixty years old and may already have been in poor health. It seems she had remained close to members of her husband's family even after his death, including his half-sister, Queen Elizabeth. An item in the queen's accounts for 11th November 1502 details a payment to William Pole, Elizabeth's Groom of the chamber 'for his costs riding from Langley to the Lady Marquess into Lincolnshire by the space of 5 days'. The accounts do not detail the reason for the trip, but perhaps he was taking her a gift of venison as was reflected in the other payments made to him that day.[3] Cecily held the manor of Multon in Lincolnshire from her Harington inheritance and it passed to her son Richard Grey in her Will after her death. As 1502 passed into 1503, Cecily had survived a whole year as a widow and perhaps may have been looking with more optimism towards the future.

As the new year dawned Cecily, along with the rest of the country, would have been shocked when they received the sad news of the death of Queen Elizabeth. Elizabeth had been a popular queen, respected by her subjects and loved by all who knew her. She had been in London where on 2nd February 1503, she had given birth to her fourth daughter, whom they named Katherine. Nine days later she had succumbed to a postpartum fever, most likely caused by an infection. The young princess Katherine also did not survive. Her son, Prince Henry, the future Henry VIII, would later go on to describe the death of his mother as being the worst day of his life. The king was bereft and retired from public life for a few weeks, lost in his own personal grief. It seems that this marriage, planned by their mothers during the darkest of days, did result in a happy union after all.

On Sunday 12th February, the day after her death, Elizabeth's coffin was carried to the Church of St Peter ad Vincula within the Tower, where she remained for the next eleven days. During that time, her coffin was watched over at all times by six ladies in rotation. Cecily may well have taken her turn in this ritual. On the day of the funeral, the queen's procession from the tower to Westminster followed the same route that she took for her coronation. Walking behind the chariot that carried the body of the queen were her four sisters, Katherine, Anne, Bridget and Cecily, all wearing mourning gowns with sweeping trains. All along the route the religious corporations, fraternities and guilds had turned out to pay their respects alongside young children dressed as angels singing psalms. The fronts of all the churches that they passed were hung with black cloth and magnificently illuminated.

After the service in Westminster Abbey, Cecily's son, Thomas Dorset, escorted the queen's sister Katherine of York, who had acted as chief mourner, and all the other lords and ladies to the queen's great chamber in the palace of Westminster where Katherine presided over a supper of fish.[4]

The unexpected death of the queen was a time for national mourning and a more individual tragedy for Cecily herself who may have developed a close friendship with her sister-in-law. But Cecily was to experience an even more personal loss a few months later in 1503 when she lost her daughter Lady Eleanor Arundell, who died aged around twenty-three, leaving behind several young children. Coming just two years after the death of her husband, this would have bought the whole family back together once more for an occasion dominated by grief and sadness, to mourn one of their own.

Having buried her eldest daughter, an act no mother ever wants to contemplate doing, Cecily must have been hoping for some respite, but fortune had not yet finished with her. Her location during Christmas 1503 is unknown, maybe she spent it with her mother, but sadly it was to be her mother's last and at some point, in early 1504, Cecily would have been delivered the devastating news of her mother's death.

Katherine Neville was around sixty-two years old when she died. She had written her Will on November 22nd 1503, perhaps signalling that she knew her health was declining. Having been married to William Hastings for nearly twenty years, Katherine never remarried after his death and remained a widow for almost as long as she had been married. Katherine and Hastings had had six children together – four boys, Edward, Richard, William and George and two daughters, Elizabeth and Anne. From Katherine's Will alone we can see the affection she had for her children and Cecily must have felt a huge grief at her passing.

In her Will Katherine requested burial not with her husband, but within the parish church of Ashby-de-la-Zouch. Given that Hastings had been laid to rest some twenty years before, it was highly unlikely that she would have been granted burial in the royal mausoleum alongside him. Instead, she chose to be laid to rest in the church that was built in the early 1470s, alongside the building work that took place during that time at their home of Ashby castle. The church is situated right next door to the castle, and an early sundial on the church tower is believed to have been viewable from the solar at the Castle. The church today contains the Hastings chapel and several memorials to later members of the family. Katherine's burial place though is in the Lady chapel.[5]

Katherine named Cecily as an executor of her Will alongside her half-brothers, Edward, Richard and William and her half-sister Anne Hastings and her husband, the Earl of Shrewsbury. She left money for a priest to sing for the souls of her father, mother and husband for the next three years and also payment to the priest who was to complete this task of six pounds per annum. She made a particular request that her priest, Sir William Englondel, be the one to take on this task if possible. Clearly a pious woman, she also left items to the chapel which included her little gilded chalice and a printed mass book.

Although many women chose not to remarry after the death of their husbands in order to retain complete control of their own finances, it seems Katherine had struggled with money and by the time of her death was not particularly well off. She was not poor by any means, but seemingly her tenants were often late in paying their rents perhaps causing her monetary worries. An arrears roll from Michaelmas 1501 indicates she was owed £23 16s 11d from five of her estates. A surviving letter from Katherine, written to Sir Reginald Grey sometime between 1496 and 1503 makes it clear she was struggling financially and also points to her failing health. She writes: 'And where I have been so long in yowre debt for you fee I besech you thenk no one unkindesse in me therefore for the cause oonly was my great disease of seleries which I have had many a daie to my great costs and charge of phisike beside odre many great charges'. She then goes on to thank him for being a good master to her son, Richard, and says she hopes to be able to pay future fees on the date they are due'.[6]

Wills are often a valuable insight into both the personal possessions of the deceased and those they were closest to during their lifetime, offering us a minute glimpse into their lives. Delving into Katherine's Will, it becomes obvious how close she was to her family and what a pious lady she was.

Still apparently owing money at the time of her death, Katherine's Will requests that all her debts are to be paid off first, including money that she had borrowed from Cecily which was to be repaid from her estate:

Item, where I owe unto Cecilie, Marquesse Dorset, certain sumes of money which I have borrowed of her at diverse times, as appeareth by bills indented thereof made, I woll that the said Cecilie, in full contentation of all such sumes of money as I owe unto her, have my bed of arres, tittor, testor, and counterpane, which she late borrowed of me, and over that, I will that she have my tabulet of gold that she now hath in her hands for a pledge, and three curtains of blew sarcionett and a traverse of blew sarcionett, and three quishions of counterfeit arres, with imagery of women, a long quishion, and two short, of blew velvet, also two carpets.

Her other children were also not forgotten. Her daughter, Anne Hastings had been married to George, Earl of Shrewsbury, who had once been a ward of the Hastings household. Katherine was seemingly very fond of him as she bequeathed to 'myne especial good Lord George, Earl of Shrewsbury, a cope of cloth of gold, of white damasce, with torpens cloth of gold and velvet upon velvet [and] a vestment of purpure velvet, with a crucifix and images of St. Peter and St. John, embroidered upon that oon of them'. Her daughter, Lady Shrewsbury, was also left a lily-embroidered cloth of gold, and other textile items including several cushions and carpets.

Edward, as the eldest son and heir, would inherit the main bulk of the Hastings estates and Cecily was required to hand over to him an image of our lady which was currently in her possession: 'Item, I bequeath to my son, Edward Lord Hastings, an image of our Lady, now being in the hands of my Lady Marquesse'. He also received his fair share of cloths, hangings, cushions and curtains as well as a third of the hay that was stored at Kirby, and all the timber that she had stored there. Edward also was allowed to keep all the bedding that he had of hers, which was in London, apart from two feather beds, a cowcher [a couch possibly], and two carpets that were to go to Richard Hastings.

Richard and William Hastings received the other two thirds of hay from Kirby and once again we can see how devout Katherine was in the items she left them which included two hangings for an altar, with the twelve Apostles embroidered with gold, with a crucifix, and the Salutation of our Lady.

They were also bequeathed 'hangings of verd that now hang in my chamber and in the parlour; alsoe all my stuffe of napree pertaining to the pantree; alsoe two pair of blankets and two pair of fustians; alsoe four pair of fine sheets; alsoe my stuffe of kitchin, as platters, dishes, sawcers, broaches, potts, and pans: alsoe all my hey that is in Lubbershorp, provided that William have more part of the hey; also two parts of the hey at Kerby; also two vestiments, two coporauxes; alsoe to Richard foure pair of brigaunters, and to William two payre, and to them both thirteen saletts'.

William Hastings also received more bedding from her chamber and some plate that was at that time in the hands of a John Holme with the instruction that he pay the said John 'at the feast of St. Andrew next coming, fifteen pounds in part of payment of a greater sum'. To her younger son, George Hastings, she left a good feather bed, a bolster, a pair of blankets, a pair of fustians and a pair of fine sheets. She also left several items to her nephews and nieces and shared out her gowns amongst her female relatives and some of her gentlewomen.

Her chaplain, Sir Christopher, was also remembered. He was to receive a vestment of crimson velvet, and a cross of black cloth of gold. She also requested that immediately after her death he entered the farm at Kerby: 'appertaining unto him, and to take all such fruits as have growne this year, with tithes, oblations, and other profits belonging to the said ferme, and over that he to perceive in money fifty-three shillings foure-pence, and to content himself for the rent of the said ferme for this year, and to pay unto the preest of Kirby his full wages unto the annuntiation of our Lady next coming'.

Lastly her household were not forgotten, she paid them their whole quarter's wages 'to be finished at Christmas next' as well as any unpaid wages due unto them. She also gave each of her gentlemen thirteen shillings four-pence, each of her yeoman were to receive ten shillings, and to every groom she bequeathed six shillings and eight-pence. To furthermore pay off any remaining debts she instructed Cecily and Edward to 'sell off hangings or bedding as shall be sold for the payment of my debts and performance of my Will'.[7]

That Katherine had a special bond with her children is demonstrated by the fact she chose them as executors of her Will 'as my special trust is in them'. That depth of feeling was obviously shared by her children. A letter written by her eldest son, Edward, who was just seventeen years old when his father was killed, illustrates how much they thought of her. In the letter, Edward writes of 'the great trouble, pains, heaviness, and labor that the said lady his mother had with him in his bringing up, and specially since the decease of his said lord and father, and the manifold motherly kindnesses to him hitherto showed'.[8] All of her children must have keenly felt her loss with Cecily perhaps as the eldest remembering the early years they shared together after the death of Cecily's father.

Unlike her mother, who chose the path of widowhood, this was not the path that Cecily would choose for herself and a year after her mother's death, in 1504, Cecily announced her intention to take a second husband. Her chosen spouse was Lord Henry Stafford, a younger son of Harry Stafford, the 2nd Duke of Buckingham and his wife, Katherine Woodville. There was a considerable age gap between them – Henry was around twenty-five years of age, with a birth date of 1479, to Cecily's forty-five. Presumably, there was an attraction between them – particularly on Cecily's side as she did not need to remarry. Henry's younger sister, Anne Buckingham would a few years later marry Cecily's nephew, George Hastings, the son of her half-brother, Edward, so perhaps the families already knew each other, and at some point an attraction naturally developed between the pair.

Their marriage most likely took place sometime in mid-1505,

as an indenture was made in April that year between Cecily Marchioness of Dorset and Lord Harry Stafford 'in consideration that he has troth plighted and promised to take her to wife'.[9] The couple needed royal permission to marry and the king gave it, although at a cost of £2000. £1000 was payable immediately, as a guarantee of Stafford's good behaviour towards his king and the second was payable over the next five years. Henry was appointed a Knight of the Order of the Garter (K.G.) the same year, perhaps intended to elevate him in status to marry Cecily.[10] As the younger Buckingham brother, he did not have any fortune or status of his own. After their father's execution at the hands of Richard III, and once Henry Tudor had taken the throne, both Henry and his elder brother Edward had been made wards of the king's mother, Margaret Beaufort. It was Edward that inherited the dukedom and all that came with it and Henry had been financially dependent on his elder brother, assisting him in managing the Stafford estates.

This intended marriage between Henry Stafford and Cecily was to cause trouble between Cecily and her family from the start. Thomas Dorset, concerned that his mother's second marriage to a much younger man would considerably diminish his inheritance, was completely against the match. This could be seen as a selfish viewpoint from her eldest son, concerned only about his own financial dealings. That may be true and he may actually have been a greedy and grasping elder son. But there may also have been an element of concern for his mother, worried perhaps that although his mother may have developed an attraction for this younger man, perhaps it was not reciprocated to the same extent by Stafford. Indeed, Thomas may have suspected, rightly or wrongly, that Stafford himself was in this just for the money. How much of that is true will never be clear, but the fact that Henry would presumably outlive Cecily due to his younger years, led to Thomas objecting that his inheritance could be diluted amongst any children that his mother and her new husband may have together. Consequently, the pair dramatically fell out over her intended nuptials and in November 1504, Thomas challenged her right to continue as his father's executor.

Tensions escalated to such a height that the king and council were forced to step in to resolve the dispute. Both Cecily and Thomas were summoned before the king so that he could resolve their differences and re-establish some sort of peace between them. They eventually reached an agreement that Cecily would receive the issues of all their lands appointed by her late husband for the performance of his Will. She would retain Astley as her dower and had to keep the Archbishop of Canterbury informed of her progress in sorting out the rest of Dorset's Will. Once this had been done, Thomas would receive his inherited lands as specified by his father and must assign her dower to her within three months of his entry. Cecily was to retain her own inherited lands for life and upon her death they would descend to Thomas and the heirs of her body. If Thomas were to die before Cecily without leaving behind any male heirs, the agreement would be null and void. If he died first but had living sons, then her lands would remain with Stafford for life, and would only pass to Thomas' sons once Henry Stafford himself had died.[11]

A further Indenture was then made in December of that year between Cecily and Stafford, which referred back to the November Indenture and added further clauses that covered what would happen in the instance of Stafford dying before Cecily:

Whereas by indenture dated 11 Nov it was agreed that Ilfardescombe manor and other lands lately recovered from her to her use for performance of her last will should descend after her death to Thomas marquis of Dorset, she now, in consideration that lord Henry Stafford has promised to marry her, grants the same for life and to the longest liver, to hold after her death to the use of lord Henry for life and thereafter to the intent that his executors shall take the issues during the feoffees' lives for performance of his Will and hers; if he predecease her, then his executors shall take the issues of Porloke, Lymyngton, Stapilton and Ichestoke Joverney manors with appurtenances in Somerset during the feoffees' lives for the performance of his Will; if the said marquis die without issue male, she grants to the above-named feoffees all her other lands etc. to hold after her death to the use of lord Henry Stafford for life (after payment of her debts) and thereafter for performance of his Will and hers.[12]

The legal wrangling between Thomas Dorset and Stafford unfortunately resulted in Cecily's daughters becoming the biggest losers in these arguments between mother and son. Their father had left them all dowries but the arguments over money caused delay in the Grey girls receiving them. One of her daughters, Dorothy, felt so aggrieved at the slow payment of her dowry, that when she married and the money was not forthcoming, she sued the executors of her father's Will for the non-payment.[13]

But despite the bickering, the wedding went ahead at some point in 1505. Cecily and Stafford would have continued to live in Cecily's properties as Stafford had none of his own and it seems Shute manor remained one of her favoured residences as in a grant made in December 1509, Stafford is referred to as 'Sir Henry Stafford, of Shute, Devon'.[14]

Settling into married life together, little is known of their movements over the next few years. But in 1509 they, like the rest of the country, would have received the news of the death of Henry VII, which occurred on 21st April. He had been on the throne for over twenty years and although perhaps the least famous of the Tudor monarchs, he was the founder of the dynasty and had changed the course of England's ruling family. Several years before, in April 1502, Prince Arthur, the king and queen's eldest son, had died at Ludlow, less than six months after his wedding to the beautiful Spanish Princess, Katherine of Aragon. The Duke of York, Prince Henry, became his father's heir upon Arthur's death, and in 1509 it was he who succeeded to the throne as Henry VIII. This new young king on the throne would eventually be a good thing for Cecily and Stafford, bringing them closer once again to court life than they perhaps had been for the past few years. But it would begin with a period of worry and uncertainty for Cecily as immediately upon Henry's accession, her husband Stafford was arrested and thrown into the tower, more on a suspicion of anything he might do than on anything he had actually done.

But what led to Stafford's committal to the tower had its origins in tensions that had begun many years before. It had begun with a younger brother of the Earl of Lincoln, Edmund de la Pole, who had taken against the king when Henry VII had refused to grant him the dukedom upon the death of his father, the Duke of Suffolk. Instead, he was only granted the lesser title of Earl of Suffolk, and Edmund had been resentful ever since. In 1498, he had been indicted of murder in a fight and fled overseas, although he was later pardoned for the offence. Returning to England for a short while, he had fled again in 1501 without royal leave, to his Aunt Margaret's court in Burgundy. In the summer of that year in what was obviously designed to be a clear threat to Henry, he began calling himself the 'White Rose'. In response to this threat, Edmund was declared an outlaw and in February 1502 many of his close associates were arrested and imprisoned, suspected of their involvement in the conspiracy. These men included James Tyrrell, William de la Pole (Edmund's younger brother), Sir John Wyndham and William Courtenay.

Thomas Dorset was also a close associate of this group of

men but for whatever reason he was not included in the 1502 arrests. However, he had clearly come under Henry's suspicion by 1508, as in that year Sir Richard Carew, who was Lieutenant of Calais, transported William Courtenay and Thomas Dorset across the sea to the Calais prison by commandment of the king. According to the writer of the Chronicle of Calais, on 18th October 1508, the pair were brought across the sea after 'they had bene in the towre of London a greate season'.[15]

The Courtenays as we know from the time of Old William Bonville, were neighbours of Cecily's in Devon. But Cecily and her family were also related to William Courtenay through marriage. In 1496, Cecily's sister-in-law, Katherine of York, had married William and they spent much of their time living at Colcombe, three miles from Shute. Katherine of York was the second youngest of the children of Edward and Elizabeth Woodville and much younger than her half-brother, Dorset. Born in 1479, she was in fact just a few years younger than her nephew, Thomas Dorset. Her husband, William Courtenay, was born in 1475 and he and Thomas Dorset had become good friends. Even after William's death in 1511, Thomas Dorset remained in touch with his aunt. Her accounts for the year 1523/24 detail payments to the servant who bought news of the Marquis' intended visit, for the carriage of wine and strawberries, and for servants who wrestled before him. Also, to the Bailiff of Sampford Peverell for bringing fish during his visit.[16] Thomas Dorset's eventual arrest was most likely due in some part to the closeness between the two families. Katherine of York did not seem to have fallen under suspicion, and neither did Cecily, although it must have been a worrying time for them both. So, it must have been even more distressing for Cecily when her husband was also arrested in 1509.

Whilst Thomas and Stafford were incarcerated, the coronation of England's new king took place. After Prince Arthur's death, his widow, Katherine of Aragon, had not returned to her Spanish homeland but had remained in England. In 1509 it was decided that she would make a suitable wife for Henry and a suitable queen for England, a role she felt had always been her destiny. In a joint coronation which took place on Midsummers Day, 24th June 1509, a newly married Henry VIII and his beautiful Spanish queen brought joy to the country. The streets of London were hung with tapestries and cloth of gold and Londoners gathered to watch this new young Tudor king take the helm of England. Henry rode to his coronation at the Abbey, and following behind him in the procession was Katherine, her long auburn hair loose, reclining in a litter. With the air still tinged with the smell of smoke from the Midsummer's eve bonfires, upon reaching the Abbey Henry and Katherine proceeded on foot through the great hall of Westminster Abbey towards the Abbey Church. The formal proceedings were followed by feasting and a great tournament that night, and the festivities then continued for two more days after. Stafford and Thomas Dorset missed the whole event. The suspicion that had fallen on both men presumably did not stretch to the whole family as some of Cecily's children were still welcome at court and Richard, John and Anthony Grey attended the coronation celebrations. Whether Cecily herself was there too is unclear.

It was not until a month later that King Henry sent to Calais for Thomas and he returned back across the channel and back into royal favour. According to the Calais chronicler, both Thomas Dorset and William Courtenay had only narrowly escaped with their lives; they had been facing execution and only survived because Henry VII had died before he could give the order.[17] Much to Cecily's relief, Stafford was also released from imprisonment and he was created Earl of Wiltshire on 27th January 1510. From then on, he would become known as Wiltshire. He very quickly became one of the king's close associates, with both men sharing a love of tournaments, hunting and lavish entertainment.[18] Both back in the centre of the court, Thomas Dorset and Wiltshire were also summoned to Henry's first parliament where Thomas carried the cap of maintenance and Wiltshire carried the sword.

With a second-generation king and queen now on the throne, the Tudor dynasty was firmly established. But even though his position was more secure than his father's had been when he first became king, Henry knew that he needed a son to carry on the royal line. After several early miscarriages, Queen Katherine gave birth to a son on New Year's Day 1511. The king was delighted. A keen jouster himself, he organised a grand tournament to be held to celebrate his son's birth. The tournament was held at Westminster in February 1511 and both Wiltshire and his stepson Dorset took part. The four knight challengers were the king himself as Ceure Loyall (Sir Loyal Heart), Sir Edward Neville as Vailliaunt Desyre, William Courtenay as Bone Valoyr and Sir Thomas Knevet as Joyous Panser. Richard Grey took part in the first day of jousting and Thomas Dorset and Wiltshire were in the lists for the second day, alongside John Grey and a new rising star at court, a certain gentleman named Thomas Boleyn.

But tragically all the hope and joy at the birth of the little prince came to a swift end when the little boy died on 22nd February. In the saddest of funerals, the little prince was laid to rest, and Thomas Dorset was honoured with the role of chief mourner. A heartbroken king and queen resolutely looked forward to any future pregnancies that they were sure would bring them a royal son and heir. Unbeknownst to anyone at this point in time, the desire for a son would go on to dominate Henry's reign and would influence many of the decisions he made throughout his life.

Little is known of Cecily and Wiltshire's life together. During their marriage, Wiltshire remained involved in court life in one way or another. He travelled to France with the king in 1513, captaining a group of 651 men and also travelled with him in 1520 for Henry's meeting with the French king at the Field of Cloth of Gold. By 1520 he had been made a privy councillor.[19] Cecily's whereabouts during those years are harder to trace. The arguments over money had not completely gone away and by 1515 Cecily and her husband were involved in another dispute with her eldest son, once again over her daughter's dowries which Thomas insisted should be paid by Cecily and Wiltshire. Her surviving daughters, Cecily, Dorothy, Mary, Elizabeth and Margaret were all in their twenties by then with Cecily the eldest at around twenty-eight and Margaret the youngest at just twenty-three. Margaret was the only one who had not married. This time their argument was arbitrated by Thomas Dorset's old schoolmaster, Thomas Wolsey. Perhaps in a show of favouritism towards his old pupil, Wolsey forced Cecily and Wiltshire to contribute rather than the money being paid from the Grey estates.[20]

In May 1521, Wiltshire was to receive bad news when his brother, Edward Stafford, the Duke of Buckingham, was arrested and tried for treason. He was arrested on charges of predicting the king's death, allegedly by listening to certain prophecies which told of the death of the king. Henry VIII was so scared of his own mortality that discussing his death in any way, shape or form was considered a treasonable offence. Thomas Dorset was on the panel that delivered the sentence, along with his brother-in-laws, Ferrers and Willoughby. He was sentenced to death. Wiltshire at this time seemingly had a good enough friendship with the king not to fall under his suspicion.

Whether Henry Stafford proved himself a good husband or not is impossible to tell, but evidently he was not good at managing his finances, which may have caused trouble within their marriage. Entries in the 1523/4 subsidy lists for Colyton, Ottery and the surrounding areas make it clear that he was considered a bad debtor. It was recorded he owed over £9 for 'fresshe a salte fyssche the whiche woll never be payde' and another lists 'my lord of wylshire ouer to her xxiiij the which she thynketh never to be paid of hit'.[21] He was even in debt to the king who had loaned him a considerable amount of money over the years, and by 1521 he owed the crown £4407 4s.[22]

By 1522, we can trace Cecily to Bedwell, the house of her daughter Dorothy and her husband Lord Mountjoy. A letter exists from that period, written from Cecily to a certain young gentleman at court named Thomas Cromwell. Before his time as Henry VIII's chief minister, Thomas Cromwell had been a lawyer and during the early 1520s, he was often contacted in that capacity. It is likely that he first became known to Cecily and her family when they required his legal help. Cecily wrote to him in August that year, addressing him as her 'sonne marquys servaunt.'[23]

Cromwell, I woll that yow send to me in hast the trussynn bed of cloth of tyssewe, and the fether bed, with the fustyons and a materas longunn to the same with the cownterpoynt; also I woll that you delyver all such tents, pavylons and hales as you have of myne to my sonne Lenard, as you tender my plesue. And thys shall be your suffycyant warrant and discharge att all tymes. Wrtytn at Bedwell thys present Thorsdaye by fore our Lady daye the Asumpcyon. Cecyl Dorsett.

Although Cecily appears to have remained close to her children, perhaps frequently visiting and staying with them as the letter from Bedwell evidences, the family disagreements rumbled on and by December 1522 another of her son in law's, John Dudley, who was married to Cecily Grey, was complaining to the king that Wiltshire was still withholding Cecily's dowry. Wiltshire responded that Dorset had failed to obey a prior agreement and requested that Wolsey make him comply. However, less than four months later, arguments between the Grey children and their stepfather ceased when Wiltshire suddenly died. Cecily had been married to him for around eighteen years.

The Earl died on 6th April 1523, aged forty-four. The couple had no children together, and with no sons to inherit the Earl of Wiltshire title, it would be held in abeyance until December 1529 when it would be awarded to Thomas Boleyn. As well as grieving for her second husband, Cecily was now tied into financial arrangements in an agreement brokered by Wolsey that she would pay her daughter's dowries out of her lands and that her younger sons would be granted a life interest in several of her properties. She also had Wiltshire's debts to repay to the king, which it was agreed she would pay back in instalments.[24]

Perhaps to assess her finances, Cecily had a survey of all her manors completed in 1525. Her surveyor, Richard Phelps made an account of all her manors in the five counties of Somerset, Devon, Cornwall, Wiltshire and Dorset. She also owned manors in other counties, including Bedfordshire, Lincolnshire, London and even as far north as Yorkshire and Cumberland, which came to her as part of the Harington fortune, but these were not included in the survey.

The survey detailed all 79 manors that she owned, which ranged from full manors of cottages and farms, to parcels of land that were worth nothing, such as 'Lords Wodde which contains 90 acres of pasture land which is worth nothing because it is full of underwood which underwood has been growing five years'. Her manors in the south-west equated to roughly 30,000 acres and had a rent roll of around £1000, with the majority of these being in Devon and Cornwall. In Cornwall she had 152 holdings, amounting to a total 3007 acres which brought in a total rent of £161.15.5 per annum. She had no free tenants. In Devon where she held the majority of her manors, the survey recorded 543 holdings, and a total of 15,841 acres. This gave her a total rent of £473.2.10 per annum and included 51 free tenants.

The majority of Cecily's properties were leased, and rent was paid either in monetary terms or sometimes in kind, for instance where her tenants promised to keep a mill in good repair or to supply Cecily with candles in lieu of their due rent. The rent for John Betiscombe for his land in Ayschelonde was one pound of pepper or 2/- yearly. For John Marschall of Meryett, he owed one sparrowhawk at Gowesbradon or 2/- yearly.

It seems Cecily was a compassionate landlady, on occasion reducing or cancelling fines and/or rent because the tenant was old as in the case of Joan Focke: 'widow holds one cottage with a small curtilage adjoining. And it is granted to her for the term of her life without a fine because she is poor and weak'. On two occasions cottage leases were granted to elderly residents who offered to pray for her.[25]

By 1527, Cecily had paid all the dowries, including to her daughter, Elizabeth, Countess of Kildare, even though she married 'without the assent of her friends, contrary to the will of the lord marquess her father, by reason whereof the said £1000 ought not to be paid'. Cecily explained she was giving Elizabeth the money nonetheless 'forasmuch as the said marriage is honourable, and I and all her friends have cause to be content with the same'.[26]

Like many other women of her time, Cecily was a pious woman and during her lifetime she made contributions to several churches, including the North aisle in Axminster church, near to Shute. During both her marriages she had spent a good proportion of her time at her manors at Shute and Wiscombe Park and must have frequented the church regularly. Wiscombe Park originally belonged to the priory of Otterton and was granted to Sir William Bonville Knight, an ancestor of Cecily's, during the reign of Henry III. During the time she and Wiltshire stayed at Wiscombe, Cecily began building the 'Dorset Aisle' at Ottery St Mary's.

The Dorset aisle is one of Cecily's most beautiful legacies

and is rich with her family connections. The Haringtons, the Staffords and the Hastings families are all represented, alongside heraldic details such as the Bourchier knot and the Wake knot (representing the families of two of her daughter's husbands) alongside the crest of Fitzgerald, Earl of Kildare, married to her daughter Elizabeth Grey.[27] There may also be a tribute to Cecily herself in the shape of the female figure in the porch who is believed to be St Cecily. The female figure carries in her hands what looks like a pair of organs, in the exact same way that St Cecilia is depicted as holding them in Raphael's celebrated drawing, engraved by Marc Antonio. The attendant angel would be that described in Chaucer's 'Seconde Nonnes tale': 'I have an angel which that loveth me, That with greet love where so I wake or slepe, is redy ay my body for to kepe'. It is though that perhaps her tenantry joined together in erecting the porch and may have had Chaucer's lines in mind, and applied them to Cecily, their beloved mistress.

In her later years Cecily also spent some of her time arranging a memorial to her beloved Elizabeth at the Church of St Dubricius in Porlock, Somerset. During Elizabeth's first marriage to Sir John Harington, the couple had a desire to build a chantry in the church at Porlock. Sir John died in 1418 and Elizabeth became Lady of the Manor of Porlock. She is referred to as Lady Elizabeth Harinton, Lady of Porlock in the Will of a John Bakelyn of Dunster in 1420.[28]

Upon Elizabeth's death the manor of Porlock fell to Cecily. In the church there are alabaster effigies to Elizabeth and John. Elizabeth is wearing a cote-hardie and gown, fastened across her chest. A double chain with an attached jewel decorates her neck and round her hips is a rich cincture. On her head she wears a horned head-dress and just over her brow is a band-coronet, studded with pearls and crested by fleurs-de-lys. Her fingers are adorned with rings. Her head rests on a cushion supported by angels and an animal rests at her feet. Lord Harington is next to her with his head resting on a helmet, adorned with a crest of a lion's head. Angels were originally on each side supporting it. He is dressed in his plate armour and his feet rest on a lion. The canopy over the effigies and the chantry and other alterations to the church were designed and added by Cecily, clearly showing her affection for Elizabeth.[29]

After Wiltshire's death, Cecily was well into the latter years of her life. The England she had been born into in the mid-1400s was long gone. By the 1520s, Henry VIII had been on the throne for over a decade. By then it had become clear that Queen Katherine was unable to provide the king with his much-desired heir. After several miscarriages and still births, Katherine had given birth to a healthy living girl in February 1516, whom they named Mary. But a further pregnancy in 1518 had culminated in the birth of another baby girl who died after only a few short hours and heralded the end of the queen's childbearing years. In 1522 the appearance at court of a young woman named Anne Boleyn had led the king to seek a divorce, enamoured with this unconventional and exotic raven-haired woman and convinced that a new wife would provide him with a son. From around 1526/1527 Henry's great matter had been rumbling away at court, with the king seeking a legal way in the eyes of the church for him to divorce his queen and marry Anne. The reason his marriage had been blighted with a lack of male heirs he decreed was because he had made a mistake in the eyes of God in marrying his brother's wife. Katherine of Aragon, arguing fiercely to retain her position as rightful queen and remain married to the man she loved, claimed that her marriage to Arthur had never been consummated and that she had therefore never fully been his wife. In November 1501 after Katherine and Arthur's wedding, Thomas Dorset had been part of the bedding ceremony, escorting the Prince to his chamber where the young couple would have been put to bed and blessed in their union, with the expectation that they would bear healthy children together. Thomas was later called to give evidence to further the king's case that Katherine's marriage had indeed been consummated. He told the court how he recalled having seen Katherine awaiting Arthur under the bedclothes during the bedding ceremony and how he had noted Arthur's healthy complexion the next day.

Cecily may have spent the last seven years after Wiltshire's death occupied with the alterations to the churches at Ottery and Porlock, as well as perhaps spending time with her children and grandchildren, and perhaps wondering, like the rest of the country, how the king's great matter would ever be resolved. However, she would not live to see the king obtain his divorce and Queen Anne Boleyn take her place alongside Henry on the throne of England as on 10th October 1530 Cecily died, aged sixty-one. It is believed she may have been in London at the time of her death, although her Will, written in 1527, had begun by specifying different burial locations which were dependent on where she was when she died. Westminster was one of the options, but she was actually buried at Astley, with her first husband, so this is perhaps an indication that she was at her home of Astley Castle when she died. However, as Astley was her preferred place of burial, it may also have been that her family transported her body to her preferred resting place next to her first husband, Dorset. Perhaps even Westminster as an option was no longer open to her when she died.

If she was in London when she died as some believe, it may have been at Shackwell in Hackney, Middlesex. Shackwell was a quiet and attractive part of Hackney, made desirable to its residents by the presence of a spring or well that provided their water. If she was there, she may have been staying in the property of a gentleman named Giles Heron, who had his seat at Shackwell. His father, Sir John Heron, a rich courtier, had died in 1522, and the manor, part of a larger estate that belonged to him, was passed down to his son Sir Giles Heron. Giles Heron is mentioned as a ffeofe in Cecily's Will so there was obviously a connection between her and the Herons.[30]

Cecily's Will was proved a month after her death, in November 1530. Following her main burial request, she was interred with Dorset in Astley:

> My body to be buried in the Chapel within the Church of the College of Astley, in Warwickshire, in the tomb where the body of the said Lord Marquess my husband is buried.
>
> I will that, soon after my decease, a thousand masses be said for my soul, in as convenient baste as may be. I will that a goodly tomb be made in the Chapel of Astley over the said Lord Marquess my husband, and another over me.[31]

Due to the large number of properties and estates she owned, and the legal obligations she was tied into, her Will is extensive. She asks for her executors to provide two priests daily to sing in the said Chapel of Astley, for the souls of her first husband and for her soul for the next eighty years. There is no mention of her second husband so perhaps that is indicative that she did not consider her marriage to him a huge success. Maybe a union based on an initial physical attraction, eventually turned into a loveless marriage with a younger man, who whittled away money like water and left her with his debts. Perhaps her son, Thomas, was astute after all?

Her daughters were then remembered, each to be left money out of her inheritance. To her sons, she left several manors: to Richard, the manor of Multon, in the county of Lincoln; to her son John the manors of Yarde, Pokin, Torrells, and Littlesdon, in the county of Somerset and to Lord Leonard Grey the manors of Says-Bonvill, and Pixton, in Somerset, and the manor of Albryngton, in Dorset, and the manor of Marston, in Sussex, for his life. Her eldest, Thomas, would of course inherit the bulk of her estates.

She also remembered her household and directed that all her servants were to be paid a years' wages plus any monies owing and instructed that if they attended her funeral, they would be expected to wear black gowns. A further £20 was to be given to poor households within four miles of the place she died. As with many last requests, she directed her executors to pay any outstanding debts out of her estate, which included the debts of her second husband, Wiltshire. Any unmade bequests from Dorset's Will that had not yet been actioned were to be performed, including giving money to the scholars of Oxford and Cambridge. Education and learning were clearly important to the family, and the time that their sons spent at Magdalen clearly impressed Dorset enough to want to contribute to the learning of other students.

Her executors were numerous and included her nephew, Henry Courtenay, Marquis of Exeter and grandson Thomas Arundell.[31] Her eldest son, Thomas Dorset, inherited the bulk of her estate, including Shute manor although interestingly was not named as an executor. Clearly their arguments over the years had clouded her view of him and she did not trust him with the important task of completing her last requests.

Today in Astley church what is thought to be her severely damaged effigy can be seen alongside those of Sir Edward Grey, Lord Ferrers of Groby and Elizabeth Talbot, although the church itself is much changed from when Thomas and Cecily were laid to rest there. Originally there were thought to be four tombs and nine alabaster effigies. The church itself was built by Sir Thomas Astley in 1343, but in 1558 Adrian Stokes, who held the estate after his wife's death, pulled down the spire and stripped the roof of lead, causing the tower to fall in the year 1600. The collapse of the tower destroyed the other monuments and is what caused the damage to Cecily's effigy. In 1607 the remains of the tower, the transepts, and the nave were demolished and the only part of the old church that remained, the old chancel, was incorporated into the nave of the newly built church. Cecily's effigy is believed to be the one on the far left of the three that remain. She is wearing a pedimental head-dress, a high-cut kirtle, cote-hardie, and mantle and at the corners are two small dogs.[32] Thomas' effigy has not survived.

Cecily Bonville Grey, the matriarch of the Grey family, had been one of the richest women in England and yet perhaps one of the least well known to us today. She has faded into the shadow of her more famous husband, yet together Cecily and Dorset went through muchand made a formidable team. Through both her marriages she led a rich and eventful life and through her children and grandchildren, her legacy continued.

Chapter Seven

Cecily's Legacy and the Nine-days Queen

The birth dates and order of the children of Cecily and Thomas Dorset are very intertwined and almost impossible to establish accurately from this distance of time. Several sources claim that Thomas Dorset, who became the second Marquis upon the death of his father was in fact the couple's third son. As they had been married since 1474, and he was not born until 1477, it is entirely possible for them to have had other sons before 1477. Edward is a name that has been mentioned more than once for their first son, and it is very possible that the couple's firstborn son would have been named Edward in honour of King Edward IV. The existence of a second son, whom may have been called Anthony according to several sources is less likely but again not impossible. That Thomas was, if not their first son, at the very least their second seems to me to be the most probable scenario, with their first son named for the king and Thomas, as their second son, after his father. But if one or even two sons did proceed Thomas, they both must have died early on, as it was Thomas Dorset who succeeded his father in 1501.

Melita Thomas in her book *The House of Grey* has made perfectly good arguments for the birth date and order of the rest of the Dorset children and I have followed her suggestive order in this book. In that suggested order we would have Thomas born c.1477 followed by Richard c.1479, John c.1481, Eleanor c.1482, Anthony c.1483, George c.1486, Cecily c.1487, Dorothy c.1488, Leonard c.1490, Mary c.1491, Elizabeth c.1492, Margaret c.1494 and Edward c.1495. Another daughter Bridget is also mentioned in several sources but if she existed at all, she must have died at a young age. The Dorsets would of course have been considerably fortunate to have all their children, bar one, reach adulthood so the possibility of Cecily having given birth to at least one or two other children who died young and went unrecorded is also very real.

After Cecily's death, her eldest son Thomas Marquis of Dorset, did not have long to enjoy his full inheritance – he died just a few months after his mother on 10th October 1530, at the age of fifty-three and was also buried in the collegiate church at Astley in Warwickshire. Inheriting both his mother and father's estates he died one of the richest men in England. In or around 1509, Thomas had married a lady named Margaret Wotton, who became Marchioness of Dorset alongside her husband. Several sources mention that Margaret may have been his second wife and that there is some evidence that he had previously been married to a lady named Eleanor Saint John, but it is unsubstantiated. During their marriage, Thomas and Margaret had eight children together, the eldest of whom was Henry Grey; he became the third Marquis of Dorset in 1530 when Thomas died.

Most of the other Grey boys were involved in the life of the court of Henry VIII to some degree or another. Richard Grey served at court and attended the funeral of Henry VII as well as the coronation festivities of Henry VIII.[1] He was very much a part of Henry VIII's court and it was the king that arranged his marriage to Florence Pudsey, Lady Clifford sometime around 1523. Richard was her third husband and her marriage to her second husband ended after she sued her husband for restitution of conjugal rights, and it came to light that she was committing adultery herself.[2] Assuming a birth date for him of c.1479, he was around forty-four years old when he married Florence, presumably prior to then preferring the life of a single man at court. They had no children together and he died in 1541, eleven years after his mother, leaving all his possessions to his wife.[3]

Sir John Grey who was born c.1481 followed in his brother's footsteps and also became part of the Henrican court. He married a lady named Elizabeth Catesby in around 1509 at the age of twenty-eight. On several ancestry sites she is named as being the daughter of Sir William Catesby by his first wife, Phillipa Bishopston. This would make her the sister of the infamous William Catesby, advisor to Richard III, and the first named in the verse that was posted on the door of St Paul's cathedral in 1484 – The Cat, the Rat and Lovell our dog, Rule all England under a Hog (the other two men were Sir Richard Ratcliffe and Sir Francis Lovell, all trusted confidants of Richard III – the hog). This seems unlikely as this Elizabeth was born in c.1438, which means by the time she married John she would have been seventy-one! John was her second husband, as she had previously married a gentleman named Roger Wake in c.1473. Elizabeth Catesby was also said to have died by 1523, when John took a second wife, Anne Barlee. The Elizabeth born in 1438 would have been a grand old age of eighty-five by then. None of this of course is impossible, but it is improbable. A more likely explanation is that she was the daughter of the same Sir William Catesby but by his second wife, Joan Barre, whom he married c.1446. This would give her a probable birth date of sometime in the mid-1450s, placing her around eighteen years of age when she married Roger and in her mid-40s when she married John. She would therefore be a half-sister of the Catesby who was an associate of Richard III. John Grey wrote a will dated 3rd March 1523[4] but was still alive when his mother died as he was left manors in Somerset for life in her Will. His second wife, Anne, is believed to have remarried in 1530 so John must also have died shortly after his mother.

Little information is available on both Anthony and George Grey. Anthony it seems also served at court with his brothers and volunteered to be part of a band of knights sent to Spain in 1511 to fight the Infidel alongside King Ferdinand. He disappears from the records before his brothers and is not mentioned in Cecily's Will, so it is probable that he died sometime in the

1520s. George Grey graduated around 1511 with a Bachelor of Civil Law and then took holy orders. He became Dean of the College of the Annunciation of St Mary in The Newarke, Leicester in 1517.[5]

Leonard Grey, born c. 1490 led a very colourful life. He was a courtier during the reign of Henry VIII and served as Lord Deputy of Ireland from 1536 to 1540. Leonard was sent to Ireland to fight against the Irish rebels, which he apparently undertook with zeal, but was accused in 1539 of allowing his sister Elizabeth›s son, the young Earl of Kildare, to escape to France when his father, Elizabeth's husband, was captured. He strongly denied the allegations but nevertheless was attainted for treason and executed on 28 July 1541 by the orders of Henry VIII. Sources differ as to whether he married once, twice or not at all.

Little is known of Edward Grey other than he was probably the couple's youngest son and that he appears to have accompanied Mary Tudor to France for her marriage to the French King Louis and he later served in her household when she returned to England and married Charles Brandon, Duke of Suffolk. Several sources say he married a lady named Anne Jerningham who served with him in the household of Brandon and Mary but again this is uncorroborated.

Out of the female Grey siblings the probable eldest, Eleanor Grey born c.1482, had of course died in 1502. She left behind at least four children, so even assuming she gave birth once a year she must have started having children in 1498. A birth date of c.1482 therefore seems fully accurate, assuming she was married by the age of fifteen, c.1497, and then went onto have four children. Her husband, John Arundell of Lanherne, Cornwall, was born in 1474 so was eight years older than her. After her death, he remarried a lady named Jane Grenville. He had two further sons with her, and a daughter, and their eldest son, Thomas, went on to marry Margaret Howard, a sister of

Queen Katherine Howard.

Mary Grey is a rather shadowy figure and seems to have stayed away from court life. Her father purchased her marriage to Sir Walter Devereux and made the final payment towards it in 1494[6] and the pair were likely married in the mid-1490s. The marriage was not initially consummated, which was understandable given that Mary was probably only around 5-6 years old at the time and her groom only three years older than that. After Dorset's death Cecily was required to buy the marriage from the king again, and alongside other executors of her husband's Will was obliged to pay £1000, £200 yearly at Hallowtide for the 'marriage of the young Lord Ferrers'.[7] Together the couple had three sons. Mary died in 1534 and is buried at St John the Baptist Church, Stowe by Charley. Her husband survived her by 24 years and went on to take a second wife, dying himself in 1558. He and his second wife are also buried with Mary in a tomb on the north wall of the chancel, under a beautiful Tudor arch.[8]

Cecily Grey, the second eldest daughter, was born c.1487 and presumably named after her mother. She lived a less than fortunate life, having been married to a gentleman named John Sutton, 3rd Baron Dudley. John Dudley was a weak man and hugely careless with money, leaving his family in financial dire straits later in life. It seems he lost pretty much everything he owned, including the family seat of Dudley Castle to his kinsman, John Dudley, Viscount Lisle, and ended up having to rely on the charity of friends. An extant letter from Cecily to Lord Cromwell written in 1539 illustrates the circumstances Cecily found herself in:

Right honourable and my singular good lord, in my most humblest wise I have me recommended unto your good lordship: glad to hear of your good health, which I pray God long to continue to his pleasure and your most heartiest desire. The cause of my writing unto you is, desiring you to be good lord unto me; it is so, as you know very well, that, by the means of my lord, my husband, I and all mine are utterly undone, unless it be the better provided by the grace of God, and likewise that it may please the king's highness to take pity of me and mine, and in that behalf, my humble desire is to your lordship to be good lord unto me, as my special trust is in you above all, next God and the king. The truth is, I have little above 20 pound a year (which I have by my lady, my mother), to find me and one of my daughters with a woman and a man to wait upon me; and surely, unless the good prioress of Nuneaton did give me meat and drink of free cost, to me and all mine that here remains with me, I could not tell what shift to make. Over and besides that, whensoever any of my children comes hither to see me, they be welcome unto the prioress as long as they list to tarry, horsemeat and man's meat, and cost them nothing, with a piece of gold or two in their purses at their departure. Wherefore in the way of charity I desire you to be good lord unto me, and to consider the poverty of me; for, if ought should come to the house of Nuneaton, I stand in a hard case, not knowing where to be, nor what shift to make, unless it may please you of your mere pity and compassion to move the king to be good and gracious unto me, according unto his most gracious pleasure to help me unto some living. Moreover, I most heartily thank your lordship of your manifold goodness showed unto my poor son Edward Dudley, for, as I perceive by him, you are special good lord unto him, specially as concerning his suit unto my lady Berkeley, not only in procurement of the king's letters, but likewise you wrote for him as instantly as though he had been your own son. Wherefore I shall daily pray for you that it may please almighty God to reward you, whereas I and my poor son am not able. Notwithstanding it may please you to consider that though you were good lord unto him, yet it was not his fortune to obtain his foresaid suit and purpose which hath been to his great cost and charge, also to his great hindrance divers ways; for all this great while he hath lived on me and other of his friends. Farther, as I perceive he hath been bold to come to dinner and supper to your lordship, by your goodness showed unto him, which hath shifted the better. Desiring you to continue your goodness unto him, considering his poverty, and mine also, I desire you to be good lord unto him in his poor suit, as I shall daily pray for your honourable lordship long to endure. Written at Nuneaton, the 24th day of February. Your daily beadwoman, Cecil Dudley. (To the Right Honourable and my singular good lord, my Lord Privy Seal)[9]

Her sister Dorothy Grey fared slightly better with her marriage. Born c.1488, she married after 1503 a gentleman named Robert Willoughby, as his second wife. His father, also named Robert was Knight of the Body to Henry VII, king's Councillor and Lord Steward of the Household. Robert Senior's cousin, Thomas Kyme, caught the eye of the queen's beautiful sister, Cecily of York in the early 1500s. Together Dorothy and Robert had two sons, Henry and William and two daughters Elizabeth and Anne. Robert died in 1521 and Dorothy remarried William Blount Lord Mountjoy (as his 4th wife) around 1523. Seven years later in 1530, her daughter Anne married Charles Blount, William's son and heir and the fifth Lord Mountjoy. Dorothy and William had further children together, a son, John, and two daughters, Mary and Dorothy. He died in 1534 and Dorothy died sometime after 1553 which is when she made her Will.[10] Assuming a correct birth date of 1488, she would have been around sixty-five when she died.

Elizabeth Grey, like her brother Leonard, led a rather colourful life mixed up with the Irish rebels. Born c.1492, she travelled to France as a young twenty-two-year-old in 1514 as

126

one of the Maids of Honour to Mary Tudor, when she became queen of France. She remained behind to serve Queen Claude when Mary returned to England, alongside Mary and Anne Boleyn. In about 1522 she became Countess of Kildare when she married Gerald FitzGerald, 9th Earl of Kildare, as his second wife. She married him either against Cecily's wishes or without her knowledge and she was said to be deeply in love with him. Later Cecily forgave her and agreed to pay her dowry. The couple had six children together, the eldest, Elizabeth, becoming a companion to the Princess Elizabeth, the daughter of Henry VIII and Anne Boleyn. Elizabeth's husband, the Earl of Kildare, was imprisoned in the Tower of London on charges of corruption and plotting rebellion in Ireland and died in 1534. Elizabeth had remained with him, nursing him throughout his imprisonment from July 1534 until his death on 12th December.

Little is known of the youngest, Margaret Grey b. c1494. She became the wife of Richard Wake Esq. and appears to have been in service to Queen Katherine.[11]

Through her marriage to Dorset, Cecily became daughter-in-law to the king and queen and entered into the sphere of the royal court. But it was her great-granddaughter who became the most famous descendant of the Greys and reached that ultimate pinnacle of power, albeit briefly. She was named Jane Grey and just over twenty years after Cecily's death, she became Queen of England for nine days.

Jane Grey was the daughter of Henry Grey, the eldest son of the second Marquis of Dorset. He had inherited the title of Marquis in 1530 when his father died and in 1531, he was created Duke of Suffolk by the king. Then in 1533 Henry Grey made a highly advantageous match when he married Francis Brandon, the daughter of the king's sister Mary Tudor and Charles Brandon and therefore a niece of Henry VIII.

After the death of his father, Henry inherited Shute manor and all his grandparents' other lands, but it was Bradgate that

Henry and Frances chose to make their family home. It was at Bradgate in 1537 that Jane Grey was born, the eldest of three daughters that would be born to the couple. Henry and his wife Frances were very much involved in court life, with Frances serving as a Lady of the Privy Chamber to Henry's sixth and last wife, Queen Katherine Parr.

Ten years later, in January 1547, King Henry VIII died and Frances retired to Bradgate with her husband. Queen Katherine Parr, now a widow, very quickly remarried. The man she took as her second husband was Sir Thomas Seymour, one of the Seymour brothers. Their sister, Jane, had been the king's third wife. By all accounts Katherine had been in love with Seymour before her marriage to the king but had had to let him go once the king had set his sights on her. The couple were married by April/May 1547 and relocated to Sudeley Castle in Gloucestershire. In February of that year, Thomas Seymour purchased Jane Grey's wardship at the cost of £2000 and she left Bradgate and went to live in the Seymour household at Sudeley.

After King Henry's death, the throne passed to his only son and heir, Prince Edward, who had been born in 1537 to Queen Jane Seymour, finally granting Henry's wish for a son to carry on the dynasty. The new king was still only a youngster himself, having been born in the same month and year as Jane Grey. Due to his age, a regency council was formed to govern the country, headed up by Edward's Uncle, Edward Seymour (brother to Thomas) and Sir John Dudley, Duke of Northumberland.

In 1553 at the age of fifteen, King Edward became ill and it soon became clear that an agreed line of succession needed to be established. As Henry VIII had advanced through one wife to another, his daughters from his first two wives, the Princesses Mary and Elizabeth, had been barred from taking the throne and Henry had never re-installed them; he had hoped right to the end that he would father more sons with his last wife, Katherine Parr. The act of succession therefore stated that if the direct line from Henry was to fail (i.e. if his only son Edward were to die) then the crown would go 'to the heirs of the body of the Lady Frances our niece, eldest daughter to our late sister the French queen lawfully begotten; and for default of such issue of the crown ... shall wholly remain and come to the heirs of the body of the Lady Eleanor, our niece, second daughter to our late sister the French queen'.[12] This plan had depended on the fact that Frances Grey would produce a male heir.

On 25 May 1553, at the age of sixteen, Jane Grey was wed to Guildford Dudley, a son of John Dudley, Duke of Northumberland. The wedding ceremony was a triple celebration and took place at Durham Place, London, the home of the Dudley family. Jane's younger sister, Katherine, and Guildford's sister, Katherine Dudley, were also married at the same time.

As King Edward's health declined, and with no heirs himself, he had to think seriously about the succession of his crown. As a protestant, Edward decided to leave his strongly catholic sister Mary out of the succession but he did have the option of re-instating his half-sister Elizabeth, the daughter of Anne Boleyn, and a protestant like himself. But as he penned his Will, he excluded both his sisters from taking the throne after him, instead making it clear that the crown was still to go to the heirs of his cousin Frances. Stating his instructions, he decreed that the crown was to be left 'to the Lady Frances's heirs male, for lack of such issue (before my death) to the Lady Janes heirs males'. If Frances had a son and he was underage at the time of Edward's death, Frances was to act as regent until he was old enough to rule. The only problem remained that as Frances was the mother of three daughters and as yet no sons, it then became dependant on Lady Jane Grey having sons.

As it became more obvious that Edward did not have long to live, the Duke of Northumberland, in his position as one of the leading men on the regency council and by then Jane's father-in-law, convinced the king to amend his Will. The clause 'Lady Janes heirs males' was changed to 'Lady Jane and her heirs males'. The addition of this one simple word pushed Jane directly in line to succeed Edward upon his death. The reason Northumberland pushed for this is not hard to fathom – once Jane was queen, his own son Guildford Dudley, as her new husband, would be ruling by her side.

On 6th July 1553 King Edward VI died and as per his amended Will, Jane Grey, Cecily and Dorset's great-granddaughter, suddenly found herself queen of England. On 10th July, Jane was carried by barge along the Thames to the Tower of London where she was crowned. For Dudley, it seemed the plan had gone rather well. But there was one small obstacle to Dudley's plan. Henry VIII's eldest daughter, Mary, a strong and proud woman, built in the mould of her mother, Katherine of Aragon, and utterly convinced of her right to be queen, was not going to take this lying down. On the same day that Jane was crowned, Mary wrote to the Privy Council asserting her 'right and title to the Crown and government of this realm'.

What Jane thought about her sudden propulsion to queenship is a bigger discussion than can be had here and is covered by some amazing authors recommended in the bibliography. It is supposed that she was a victim of those adults around her, who used her as a pawn in their games to gain power and this is probably in part true. But Jane did have a strength running through her and once she became queen, she quickly informed her father-in-law that Guildford Dudley would not serve as king beside her. The fact that she was prepared to stand up to these powerful men may have made her a great leader if she had been given the chance. But it was never going to be.

The Catholic Mary was hugely popular with the people, who had taken Katherine of Aragon to their hearts and had done the same with her daughter, Mary. As she raised her army and set off from her base of Framlingham Castle in Norfolk, heading towards London, many of the nobility who had supported Jane initially, began to retreat. In the end there was no need for battle. On 19th July, the Earl of Pembroke rode into Cheapside to proclaim Mary as queen of England and met with no resistance. All those who had supported Jane disappeared and Jane herself was moved from her royal apartments in the tower to free them up for England's new queen. Jane had ruled England for just nine days. She was housed in another set of rooms in the tower to await her fate and her husband, Guildford Dudley was also captured and held in the tower.

In the days that followed, Jane's mother, Frances, met with Queen Mary en route to the capital and begged for her family to be spared. Her words must have had some effect and Jane's father, Henry Grey, was pardoned. Jane, however, was charged with treason. Queen Mary eventually arrived in London on 3rd August and Jane's father-in-law, John Dudley, Earl of Northumberland, was executed for treason just under three weeks later.

Jane herself wrote to Mary from the tower and although she would not free her, Mary demonstrated some compassion towards her cousin and agreed she would spare her life. But a few months later, in early 1554, her foolish father, Henry Grey, led another rebellion. This time the rebels planned to remove Mary from the throne and replace her with her protestant sister, Elizabeth. They failed in their task, and although his plan had not this time involved his daughter, Jane, Mary was persuaded by her councillors that allowing her to live would prove a continual threat to her queenship. On 12th February 1554 first Guildford and then Jane were led to the executioner's block. Carrying her prayer book, Jane gave a brave speech for a young girl who was just seventeen years old, and the executioner ended her short life. Henry Grey was executed eleven days later and all his properties, including Cecily's beloved Shute, were confiscated by the state.

It was a tragic end to a branch of the Grey dynasty that was begun so successfully by Thomas and Cecily through their union in 1474. Other Grey family members of course went on to lead fulfilling lives, but the riches and manors held by the family during the late 1400s and early 1500s disappeared when instead of living alongside the crown, her grandson rebelled against it.

References

Chapter One

1. Blacman, John. *Henry the Sixth, a reprint of John Blacman's memoir (with translation and notes by M.R. James)*. Cambridge University Press, 1919.

2. Bridie, M.F. *The Story of Shute*. Shute School Ltd, Axminster, 1955.

3. Rogers, William Henry Hamilton. *The Strife of the Roses and Days of the Tudors in the West*. Project Gutenberg, 3rd June 2010.

4. *The Croyland Chronicle*. (Note the writer incorrectly names Lord Harington as Robert).

5. Ibid.

6. The History of Parliament: The House of Commons 1386-1421, ed. J.S. Roskell, L. Clark, C. Rawcliffe., Boydell and Brewer, 1993.

7. Baldwin, David. *The Kingmakers' Sisters*. The History Press, 2009.

8. The History of Parliament: The House of Commons 1386-1421, ed. J.S. Roskell, L. Clark, C. Rawcliffe., Boydell and Brewer, 1993.

9. Rogers, William Henry Hamilton. *The Strife of the Roses and Days of the Tudors in the West*. Project Gutenberg, 3rd June 2010.

10. Thomas, Melita. *The House of Grey: Friends and Foes of Kings*. Amberley Publishing, 2019.

11. Bridie, M.F. *The Story of Shute*. Shute School Ltd, Axminster, 1955.

12. Orme, Nicholas. *Medieval Children*. Yale University Press, 2003.

Chapter Two

1. Richardson, Douglas. *Magna Carta Ancestry: a study in colonial and medieval families.* Genealogical Publishing Company, 2005.
2. Ibid.
3. Steward, Desmond. *The Wars of the Roses.* Robinson, 2007.
4. Ibid.
5. Ibid.
6. www.gatehouse-gazetteer.info
7. Steward, Desmond. *The Wars of the Roses.* Robinson, 2007.
8. Baldwin, David. *The Kingmakers' Sisters.* The History Press, 2009.
9. Ibid.
10. More, Thomas (Logan, George Ed.). *The History of King Richard III.* Indiana University Press, 2005.
11. Thomas, Melita. *The House of Grey: Friends and Foes of Kings.* Amberley Publishing, 2019.
12. Jones, Dan. *The Hollow Crown: The Wars of The Roses and the Rise of the Tudors.* Faber & Faber, 2015.
13. Richardson, Douglas. *Magna Carta Ancestry: a study in colonial and medieval families.* Genealogical Publishing Company, 2005.
14. Licence, Amy. *Edward IV and Elizabeth Woodville.* Amberley Publishing, 2016.
15. Steward, Desmond. *The Wars of the Roses.* Robinson, 2007.
16. Ibid
17. Richardson, Douglas. *Magna Carta Ancestry: a study in colonial and medieval families.* Genealogical Publishing Company, 2005.
18. Orme, Nicholas. *Medieval Children.* Yale University Press, 2003.
19. Sandeman, G.A.C. *Calais Under English Rule.* BH Blackwell, Oxford, 1908.
20. Richardson, Douglas. *Magna Carta Ancestry: a study in*

colonial and medieval families. Genealogical Publishing Company, 2005.

21. Gairdner James (ed.). *The Paston Letters, A.D. 1422-1509. Vol. V.* Project Gutenberg.

22 Sandeman, G.A.C. *Calais Under English Rule*. BH Blackwell, Oxford, 1908.

23. English Heritage (www.english-heritage.org.uk)

24. Canto, Leonard M. *The medieval castles of Leicestershire. Transactions of the Leicestershire Archaeological and Historical Society.*

25. Woolnoth, William. *The ancient castles of England and Wales, engraved. by W. Woolnoth, with historical descriptions by EW Brayley.* Longman, Hursts, London, 1825.

Chapter Three

1. Richardson, Douglas. *Magna Carta Ancestry: a study in colonial and medieval families*. Genealogical Publishing Company, 2005.

2. Thomas, Melita. *The House of Grey: Friends and Foes of Kings.* Amberley Publishing, 2019.

3. Richardson, Douglas. *Magna Carta Ancestry: a study in colonial and medieval families*. Genealogical Publishing Company, 2005.

4. Thomas, Melita. *The House of Grey: Friends and Foes of Kings.* Amberley Publishing, 2019.

5. *The Boke of Noblesse: Addressed to King Edward the Fourth on His Invasion of France in 1475*. With an Introduction by John Gouch Nichols, FSA. Roxburghe Club, 1860. Project Gutenberg.

6. Leland, John. *The itinerary of John Leland in or about the years 1535-1543*. Edited by Lucy Toulmin Smith. G. Bell 1906.

7. Stoate, T.L. *A Survey of West Country Manors, 1525: The Lands of the Marchioness of Dorset, Lady Harrington and Bonville in Cornwall, Devon, Dorset, Somerset and Wiltshire.*

BD Welchman, 2003.

8. Bridie, M.F. *The Story of Shute*. Shute School Ltd, Axminster, 1955.

9. Penn, Thomas. *The Brothers York: An English Tragedy*. Penguin Books, 2020.

10. Gairdner James (ed.). *The Paston Letters, A.D. 1422-1509, Vol. V*. Project Gutenberg. (See chapter chapter seven for a discussion on the birth order of the Grey children).

11. Nicol, W. *Illustrations of Ancient State and Chivalry: From Manuscripts Preserved in the Ashmolean Museum; with an Appendix*. Roxburghe Club, Ashmolean Museum, January 1840. Shakespeare Press.

12. Ibid.

13. Ibid.

14. Thomas, Melita. *The House of Grey: Friends and Foes of Kings*. Amberley Publishing, 2019.

15. Kingsford, Charles Lethbridge (editor). *The Stonor letters and papers, 1290-1483*. Ed. for the Royal historical society, from the original documents in the National Archives.

16. Toumlin, Joshua. *The History of the Town of Taunton in the Country of Somerset*. 1791.

17. Daniel Lysons and Samuel Lysons, Magna Britannia: Volume 6, Devonshire. London, 1822. British History Online.

Chapter Four

1. More, Thomas (Logan, George Ed.). *The History of King Richard III*. Indiana University Press, 2005.

2. Crossland, Margaret. *The Life and Legend of Jane Shore, The Mysterious Mistress*. Sutton Publishing, 2006.

3. Sutton and Visser-Fuch, *Royal Funerals of the House of York at Windsor*. Richard III Society, 2005.

4. Ibid

5. Croyland Chronicle

6. Vergil, Polydore (Ellis, Sir Henry Ed.). *Three books of Polydore Vergil's English history, comprising the reigns of Henry VI., Edward IV., and Richard III.* from an early translation, preserved among the mss. of the old royal library in the British museum. Printed for the Camden Society, JB Nichols & Sons, 1844.

7. Jones, Dan. *The Hollow Crown: The Wars of The Roses and the Rise of the Tudors.* Faber & Faber, 2015.

8. Ibid

9. More, Thomas (Logan, George Ed.). *The History of King Richard III.* Indiana University Press, 2005.

10. Bell, Henry Nugent. *The Huntingdon Peerage (Comprising a Detailed Account of the Evidence and Proceedings Connected with the Recent Restoration of the Earldom ... to which is Prefixed a Genealogical and Biographical History of the Illustrious House of Hastings, Including a Memoir of the Present Earl and His Family).* Baldwin, Craddock and Joy, 1820.

11. Ibid

12. Ibid

13. Ibid

14. Wood, Cindy. *The Chantries and Chantry Chapels of St George's Chapel, Windsor Castle.* Academia Paper.

15. www.stgeorges-windsor.org

16. Bell, Henry Nugent. *The Huntingdon Peerage (Comprising a Detailed Account of the Evidence and Proceedings Connected with the Recent Restoration of the Earldom ... to which is Prefixed a Genealogical and Biographical History of the Illustrious House of Hastings, Including a Memoir of the Present Earl and His Family).* Baldwin, Craddock and Joy, 1820.

17. Crossland, Margaret. *The Life and Legend of Jane Shore, The Mysterious Mistress.* Sutton Publishing, 2006.

18. Pisan, Christine. *The Treasure of the City of Ladies.* Penguin Classics, 2003.

Chapter Five

1. Crossland, Margaret. *The Life and Legend of Jane Shore, The Mysterious Mistress.* Sutton Publishing, 2006.
2. More, Thomas (Logan, George Ed.). *The History of King Richard III.* Indiana University Press, 2005.
3. Richardson, Douglas. *Magna Carta Ancestry: a study in colonial and medieval families.* Genealogical Publishing Company, 2005.
4. Leland, *Joannis Lelandi Antiquarii de rebus Britannicis Collectanea (Vol. 5).* Thomas Hearne, 1770.
5. Ibid
6. Ibid.
7. Bacon, Francis. *History of Reign of King Henry VII.* 1622.
8. Leland, *Joannis Lelandi Antiquarii de rebus Britannicis Collectanea (Vol. 5).* Thomas Hearne, 1770.
9. Thomas, Melita. *The House of Grey: Friends and Foes of Kings.* Amberley Publishing, 2019.
10. www.historicengland.org.uk
11. www.groby.org.uk (research by David Ramsey, initiated by the Time Team Dig at Groby in 2010).
12. National Archives (www.nationalarchives.gov.uk) CI chancery proceedings (before 1558). Ref: 1502/16.
13. Elwes, Dudley George Cary and Robinson, Charles J. *A History of the Castles, Mansions and Manors of West Sussex.* London, Longmans & Co, 1876.
14. Sutton and Visser-Fuch, *Royal Funerals of the House of York at Windsor.* Richard III Society, 2005.
15. Thomas, Melita. *The House of Grey: Friends and Foes of Kings.* Amberley Publishing, 2019.
16. Ibid.
17. Davidson, James. *The History of Newenham Abbey, in the County of Devon.* Longman & Co., London, 1843.
18. Tudor Chamber Books Online: BL Add MS 7099 folio 24 (Payments), 1495.

19. Bloxam, John Rouse. *A Register of the Presidents, Fellows, Demies, Instructors in Grammar and in Music, Chaplains, Clerks, Choristers, and Other Members of Saint Mary Magdalen College in the University of Oxford, From the Foundation of the College to the Present Time.* The Demies. Volume 1.

20. Smith. Goldwin. Oxford and her Colleges. Macmillan & Company, 1894.

21. Bloxam, John Rouse. *A Register of the Presidents, Fellows, Demies, Instructors in Grammar and in Music, Chaplains, Clerks, Choristers, and Other Members of Saint Mary Magdalen College in the University of Oxford. From the Foundation of the College to the Present Time.* Volume 3.

Chapter Six

1. Thomas, Melita. *The House of Grey: Friends and Foes of Kings.* Amberley Publishing, 2019.

2. Ibid.

3. Nicolas, Sir Nicholas Harris. *Privy purse expenses of Elizabeth of York; Wardrobe Accounts of Edward the Fourth. With a memoir of Elizabeth of York.* Sir Nicholas Harris. William Pickering, 1830.

4. Weir, Alison. *Elizabeth of York: The First Tudor Queen.* Vintage, 2014.

5. www.sthelensashby.net

6. Baldwin, David. *The Kingmakers' Sisters.* The History Press, 2009.

7. Bell, Henry Nugent. *The Huntingdon Peerage (Comprising a Detailed Account of the Evidence and Proceedings Connected with the Recent Restoration of the Earldom ... to which is Prefixed a Genealogical and Biographical History of the Illustrious House of Hastings, Including a Memoir of the Present Earl and His Family).* Baldwin, Craddock and Joy, 1820.

8. Harris, *English Aristocratic Women, 1450-1550: Marriage and Family, Property and Careers.* Oxford University Press, 2002.

9. CCR Henry VII vol.2 Sealed 4 Dec., 20 Henry VII. English. (Ref: 478)

10. Dockray, Keith. *Stafford, Henry, Earl of Wiltshire*. Oxford DNB, 2004.

11. CCR Henry VII vol.2. Sealed 11 Nov., 20 Henry VII. English. 11th November 1504. (Ref: 414)

12. CCR Henry VII vol.2 Sealed 4 Dec., 20 Henry VII. English. (Ref: 435)

13. National Archives (www.nationalarchives.gov.uk) CI chancery proceedings (before 1558). Ref: 312/98.

14. 'Henry VIII: December 1509', in Letters and Papers, Foreign and Domestic, Henry VIII, Volume 1, 1509-1514, ed. J S Brewer (London, 1920), pp. 127-144. British History Online http://www.british-history.ac.uk/letters-papers-hen8/vol1/pp127-144.

15. Turpyn, Richard (editor). *The Chronicle of Calais: In the Reigns of Henry VII. and Henry VIII. to the Year 1540*. Edited from a Mss. in the British Museum. Camden Society, January 1846.

16. *Tudor and Stuart Devon: The Common Estate and Government*: Essays presented to Joyce Younings. Todd Grey, Margery M. Rowe, Audrey M. Erskine. University of Exeter Press, 1992.

17. Turpyn, Richard (editor). *The Chronicle of Calais: In the Reigns of Henry VII. and Henry VIII. to the Year 1540*. Edited from a Mss. in the British Museum. Camden Society, January 1846.

18. Dockray, Keith. *Stafford, Henry, Earl of Wiltshire*. Oxford DNB, 2004.

19. Ibid.

20. Thomas, Melita. *The House of Grey: Friends and Foes of Kings*. Amberley Publishing, 2019.

21. Amery, John S. *Devon and Cornwall Notes and Queries*. Volume XI. James G. Commin, 1921.

22. Dockray, Keith. *Stafford, Henry, Earl of Wiltshire*. Oxford DNB, 2004.

23. Merriman, Roger Bigelow. *Life and Letters of Thomas Cromwell*. Vol. I. Oxford at the Clarendon Press, 1902.
24. Harris, *English Aristocratic Women, 1450-1550: Marriage and Family, Property and Careers*. Oxford University Press, 2002.
25. Stoate, T.L. *A Survey of West Country Manors, 1525: The Lands of the Marchioness of Dorset, Lady Harrington and Bonville in Cornwall, Devon, Dorset, Somerset and Wiltshire*. BD Welchman, 2003.
26. Harris, *English Aristocratic Women, 1450-1550: Marriage and Family, Property and Careers*. Oxford University Press, 2002.
27. Dalton, John Neale. *The Collegiate Church of Ottery St. Mary: being the Ordinacio et Statuta, Ecclesie Sancte Marie de Otery, Exon. Diocesis A.D. 1338, 1339*. Ed. from the Exeter Chapter MS. 3521, and the Winchester Cartulary vol. 1. part ii.ff.98-114, with plans, photographs, introduction and notes by Ottery St. Mary (England). 1917.
28. Hook, Walter. *A History of the Ancient Church of Porlock and of the Patron Saint, St. Dubricius, and his Times*. 1893.
29. Rogers, William Henry Hamilton. *The Strife of the Roses and Days of the Tudors in the West*. Project Gutenberg, 3rd June 2010.
30. 'Hackney: Shacklewell', in A History of the County of Middlesex: Volume 10, Hackney, ed. T F T Baker (London, 1995), pp. 35-38. British History Online http://www.british-history.ac.uk/vch/middx/vol10/pp35-38.
31. Nicolas, N.H. *Testamenta vetusta: illustrations from wills, of manners, customs, &c., from the reign of Henry the second to queen Elizabeth*. Vol. 2. 1826.
32. *A History of the County of Warwick: Volume 6, Knightlow Hundred*. Originally published by Victoria County History, London, 1951.

Chapter Seven

1. Thomas, Melita. *The House of Grey: Friends and Foes of Kings*.

Amberley Publishing, 2019.

2. Thornton, Tim and Carlton, Katherine. *The Gentleman's Mistress – Illegitimate Relationships and Their Children, 1450-1640*. Manchester University Press, 2019.

3. Nicolas, N.H. *Testamenta vetusta: illustrations from wills, of manners, customs, &c., from the reign of Henry the second to queen Elizabeth*. Vol. 2. 1826.

4. Richardson, Douglas. *Magna Carta Ancestry: a study in colonial and medieval families*. Genealogical Publishing Company, 2005.

5. Thomas, Melita. *The House of Grey: Friends and Foes of Kings*. Amberley Publishing, 2019.

6. Tudor Chamber Books: E101/413/2/2 folio 77r (Receipts), 1494

7. Tudor Chamber Books: BL Add MS 21480 folio 100r (Obligations), 1503

8. www.midtrentchurches.org.uk

9. Green, Mary Anne Everett. *Letters of Royal and Illustrious Ladies of Great Britain, From the Commencement of the Twelfth Century to the Close of the Reign of queen Mary*. Vol 3.

10. Richardson, Douglas. *Magna Carta Ancestry: a study in colonial and medieval families*. Genealogical Publishing Company, 2005.

11. Thomas, Melita. *The House of Grey: Friends and Foes of Kings*. Amberley Publishing, 2019.

12. Watkins, Sarah-Beth, *The Tudor Brandons*, Chronos Books, 2020.

Select Bibliography

Cecily Grey does not feature heavily in many books. But to give you a feel for the period she lived in and the lives of those she knew, the following books are recommended reads.

Baldwin, David, *Elizabeth Woodville, Mother of the Princes in the Tower*, Sutton Publishing, 2002.

Baldwin, David, *The Kingmakers' Sisters*, The History Press, 2009.

Bell, Henry Nugent, *The Huntingdon Peerage (Comprising a Detailed Account of the Evidence and Proceedings Connected with the Recent Restoration of the Earldom ... to which is Prefixed a Genealogical and Biographical History of the Illustrious House of Hastings, Including a Memoir of the Present Earl and His Family.*, Baldwin, Craddock and Joy, 1820.

Bridie, M.F, *The Story of Shute*, Shute School Ltd, Axminster, 1955.

Crossland, Margaret, *The Life and Legend of Jane Shore, The Mysterious Mistress*, Sutton Publishing, 2006.

Harris, Barbara J., *English Aristocratic Women, 1450-1550: Marriage and Family, Property and Careers*, Oxford University Press, 2002.

Hicks, Michael, *The Family of Richard III*, Amberley Publishing, 2015.

Higginbotham, Susan, *The Woodvilles*, The History Press, 2013.

Hodder, Sarah J. *The Queen's Sisters: The Lives of the Sisters of Elizabeth Woodville*, John Hunt Publishing, 2020.

Hodder, Sarah J. *The York Princesses*, John Hunt Publishing, 2021.

Jones, Dan, *The Hollow Crown: The Wars of the Roses and the Rise of the Tudors*, Faber & Faber, 2014.

Leyser, Henrietta, *Medieval Women: A Social History of Women in England 450-1500*, W&N, 2005.

Licence, Amy, *Edward IV and Elizabeth Woodville*, Amberley

Publishing, 2016.

Licence, Amy, *Elizabeth of York – Forgotten Tudor Queen*, Amberley Publishing, 2013.

Lisle, Leanda de., *The Sisters Who Would Be Queen – The Tragedy of Mary, Katherine and Lady Jane Grey*, Harper Press, 2010.

Macgibbon, David, *Elizabeth Woodville – A Life: The Real Story of the White Queen*, 2013.

Okerlund, A., *Elizabeth of York*, Palgrave Macmillan, 2009.

Penn, Thomas, *The Brothers York: An English Tragedy*, Penguin Books, 2020.

Plowden, Alison. *Lady Jane Grey: Nine Days Queen*, The History Press, 2004.

Steward, Desmond, *The Wars of the Roses*, Robinson, 2007.

Sutton and Visser-Fuch, *Royal Funerals of the House of York at Windsor*, Richard III Society, 2005.

Tallis, Nicola, *Crown of Blood: The Deadly Inheritance of Lady Jane Grey*, Michael O'Mara, 2017.

Thomas, Melita, *The House of Grey: Friends and Foes of Kings*, Amberley Publishing, 2019.

Watkins, Sarah-Beth, *The Tudor Brandons*, Chronos Books, 2020.

Weir, Alison, *Lancaster and York*, Vintage, 2009.

CHRONOS
BOOKS

HISTORY

Chronos Books is an historical non-fiction imprint. Chronos publishes real history for real people; bringing to life people, places and events in an imaginative, easy-to-digest and accessible way - histories that pass on their stories to a generation of new readers.
If you have enjoyed this book, why not tell other readers by posting a review on your preferred book site.

Recent bestsellers from Chronos Books are:

Lady Katherine Knollys
The Unacknowledged Daughter of King Henry VIII
Sarah-Beth Watkins
A comprehensive account of Katherine Knollys' questionable
paternity, her previously unexplored life in the Tudor court
and her intriguing relationship with Elizabeth I.
Paperback: 978-1-78279-585-8 ebook: 978-1-78279-584-1

Cromwell was Framed
Ireland 1649
Tom Reilly
Revealed: The definitive research that proves the Irish nation
owes Oliver Cromwell a huge posthumous apology for
wrongly convicting him of civilian atrocities in 1649.
Paperback: 978-1-78279-516-2 ebook: 978-1-78279-515-5

Why The CIA Killed JFK and Malcolm X
The Secret Drug Trade in Laos
John Koerner
A new groundbreaking work presenting evidence that the CIA
silenced JFK to protect its secret drug trade in Laos.
Paperback: 978-1-78279-701-2 ebook: 978-1-78279-700-5

The Disappearing Ninth Legion
A Popular History
Mark Olly
The Disappearing Ninth Legion examines hard evidence for the
foundation, development, mysterious disappearance, or possi-
ble continuation of Rome's lost Legion.
Paperback: 978-1-84694-559-5 ebook: 978-1-84694-931-9

Beaten But Not Defeated
Siegfried Moos - A German anti-Nazi who settled in Britain
Merilyn Moos
Siegi Moos, an anti-Nazi and active member of the German
Communist Party, escaped Germany in 1933 and, exiled in
Britain, sought another route to the transformation
of capitalism.
Paperback: 978-1-78279-677-0 ebook: 978-1-78279-676-3

A Schoolboy's Wartime Letters
An evacuee's life in WWII — A Personal Memoir
Geoffrey Iley
A boy writes home during WWII, revealing his own fascinating
story, full of zest for life, information and humour.
Paperback: 978-1-78279-504-9 ebook: 978-1-78279-503-2

The Life & Times of the Real Robyn Hoode
Mark Olly
A journey of discovery. The chronicles of the genuine historical
character, Robyn Hoode, and how he became one of England's
greatest legends.
Paperback: 978-1-78535-059-7 ebook: 978-1-78535-060-3

Readers of ebooks can buy or view any of these bestsellers by clicking on the live link in the title. Most titles are published in paperback and as an ebook. Paperbacks are available in traditional bookshops. Both print and ebook formats are available online.

Find more titles and sign up to our readers' newsletter at http://www.johnhuntpublishing.com/history-home

Follow us on Facebook at https://www.facebook.com/ChronosBooks

and Twitter at https://twitter.com/ChronosBooks